KT-195-376

Advance Praise from the field

The
Heart
of
Change

"A fantastic piece of work."

—Carl Frattini, Business Manager, Electric Systems,
United Illuminating Company, Shelton, CT

"A powerful message, communicated with great effectiveness."

—Ho-il Kim, Vice President and General Counsel, Cabot Corporation,
Boston, MA

"A new message, a rare case where a book offers something that has not been
said before."

—Alan Frohman, Founder and Executive Partner, Lexington
Leadership Partners, Lexington, MA

"By and large, there is no lack of analytics, decision trees, financial models, process maps, and other forms of logical intercourse within corporate
America. Our days are saturated with rational, left-brain thought patterns.
This book does an excellent job of helping us where we need it most—on
the emotional or passionate side of the equation for driving change."

—Gjon Nivica Jr., Vice President and General Counsel, Engines &
Systems, Honeywell International, Inc., Phoenix, AZ

"A lovely book. The use of stories makes [the authors'] ideas about the
change process so real and so tangible."

—Scott Jamieson, President, The Care of Trees, Wheeling, IL

"The presentation is most compelling. The emotional content, the stories with heart, will win over even the most skeptical reader."

> —Bo Thomas, Company Leader and Owner, The Thomas Consulting Group, Little Rock, AR

"The heart-emotions theme blends effectively with the otherwise hard mechanics of some of the eight steps of leading change. The stories provide strong examples of the concepts and best practices. The 'What Works' and 'What Does Not Work' segments throughout the book summarize each section well. The overall results are excellent."

> —Robert Bender, Senior Operations Coordinator, Northrop Grumman, Newport News, VA

"Entertaining, highly readable, and very useful."

> —Peter Wood, State Manager, Walter Construction Group Ltd., Brisbane, Australia

"The illustrations, metaphors, and analogies provide mental pictures that clarify the concepts. Using the right-brain and left-brain approach, the book assists readers to understand both intellectually and emotionally. I am left feeling that if I become stuck in the change process, I can refer to a specific chapter and reread the conceptual information as well as the illustrative stories. Overall, this strikes me as a sort of right-brain field manual for implementing Kotter's left-brain *Leading Change*."

> —Jim Williams, High School Principal, Paxon School for Advanced Studies, Jacksonville, FL

"A joy to read and to learn from."

> —Sidharth Birla, Chairman, Xpro India, Limited, New Delhi, India

"*The Heart of Change* is extremely well done. It has all of the elements necessary to be a highly useful tool for those who wish to make change happen."

> —Paul Daulerio, President, Founder, and CEO, Organization Plus, Inc., Weston, CT

"It's a great book. I have already successfully used the storytelling approach right in the middle of a major restructuring when people were asking 'Remind me again why we are doing this?'"

—David Bening, VP and General Manager, General Polymers, Ashland Distribution Co., Dublin, OH

"More pragmatic than other change books. It offers clear advice. I have already made it required reading for my direct reports."

—Dan Sajkowski, Optimization Manager, BP Amoco PLC, Whiting, NH

"The individual case histories contain many pragmatic suggestions that can be readily applied to a reader's organization. For the action-oriented manager, it's excellent reading."

—Doug Reid, Senior Vice President, Human Resources, PanAm Satellite, Wilton, CT

"The concept is brilliant. I found myself highlighting all kinds of ideas that I can put to use in my job *now*."

—Mary Thomas, Program Manager, U.S. Army, Alexandria, VA

"The material has broad relevance—to individual contributors as well as managers and executives. The benefits to all come quickly in what is a very easy read."

—Charles Doucot, General Manager, Technical Computing, Hewlett-Packard Co., Burlington, MA

"It does not matter whether you are the one in charge, an active agent, or if you consider yourself a passive sufferer of change in your organization. In every case, the book reflects the reality you are living, and enables you to gain some control over it and better manage your part."

—Susanna Martin, General Manager, L'Alianca, Barcelona, Spain

"I hate business books. I usually cannot make it past the first twenty pages. I read to the end of *The Heart of Change* with great pleasure. It's the ultimate study of effective change management and leadership."

—Jean-Rene Gougelet, CEO, Mikasa, Inc., Secaucus, NJ

"An excellent book on a topic that is so important in today's business climate."

—David Walsh, Vice President of Classified Services, *Chicago Tribune,* Chicago, IL

"A very enjoyable book."

—Jeff Kishel, Vice President, MWH Americas, Inc., Sacramento, CA

"Powerful and very useful."

—John Strauss, CEO, Ocean Design, Inc., Ormand Beach, FL

"Outstanding book."

—Ben Anderson-Ray, Private Investor and Consultant, Sunrise Medical, Inc., Rancho Santa Fe, CA

"Inspiring."

—Lee Smedley, Principal, Smedley Consulting, Shoemakersville, PA

The
HTheeart
of
Change

REAL-LIFE STORIES OF HOW PEOPLE
CHANGE THEIR ORGANIZATIONS

John P. Kotter

Dan S. Cohen

HARVARD BUSINESS SCHOOL PRESS

Boston, Massachusetts

Copyright 2002 John P. Kotter and Deloitte Consulting LLC
All rights reserved
Printed in the United States of America
10 09 08 07   11 10 9 8

Requests for permission to use or reproduce material from this book should be directed to permissions@hbsp.harvard.edu, or mailed to Permissions, Harvard Business School Publishing, 60 Harvard Way, Boston, Massachusetts 02163.

The authors are in no way affiliated with Heart of Change; Change of Heart Associates, of Baldwinsville, New York.

978-1-57851-254-6 (ISBN 13)

Library of Congress Cataloging-in-Publication Data

Kotter, John P., 1947-
  The heart of change : real-life stories of how people change
their organizations / John P. Kotter, Dan S. Cohen.
      p. cm.
Includes index.
  ISBN 1-57851-254-9 (alk. paper)
  1. Organizational change. I. Cohen, Dan S. II. Title.
  HD58.8 .K645 2002
  658.4'06—dc21

                                        2002001475

The paper used in this publication meets the requirements of the American National Standard for Permanence of Paper for Publications and Documents in Libraries and Archives Z39.48-1992.

To Nancy and Ronnie
who have been at the heart
of our changes

CONTENTS

STEP 2

Build the Guiding Team   37

Helping pull together the right group of people with the right characteristics and sufficient power to drive the change effort. Helping them to behave with trust and emotional commitment to one another.

STEP 3

Get the Vision Right   61

Facilitating the movement beyond traditional analytical and financial plans and budgets. Creating the right compelling vision to direct the effort. Helping the guiding team develop bold strategies for making bold visions a reality.

STEP 4

Communicate for Buy-In   83

Sending clear, credible, and heartfelt messages about the direction of change. Establishing genuine gut-level buy-in that shows up in how people act. Using words, deeds, and new technologies to unclog communication channels and overcome confusion and distrust.

STEP 5

Empower Action   103

Removing barriers that block those who have genuinely embraced the vision and strategies. Taking away sufficient obstacles in their organizations and in their hearts so that they behave differently.

STEP 6

Create Short-Term Wins 125

Generating sufficient wins fast enough to diffuse cynicism, pessimism, and skepticism. Building momentum. Making sure successes are visible, unambiguous, and speak to what people deeply care about.

STEP 7

Don't Let Up 143

Helping people create wave after wave of change until the vision is a reality. Not allowing urgency to sag. Not ducking the more difficult parts of the transformation, especially the bigger emotional barriers. Eliminating needless work so you don't exhaust yourself along the way.

STEP 8

Make Change Stick 161

Ensuring that people continue to act in new ways, despite the pull of tradition, by rooting behavior in reshaped organizational culture. Using the employee orientation process, the promotions process, and the power of emotion to enhance new group norms and shared values.

CONCLUSION

We See, We Feel, We Change 179

Feeling and thinking. The need for more than a few heroes in a turbulent world.

PREFACE

Six years ago I wrote a book entitled *Leading Change*. It looked at what people actually did to transform their organizations to make them winners in an increasingly turbulent world. By *transform*, I mean the adoption of new technologies, major strategic shifts, process reengineering, mergers and acquisitions, restructurings into different sorts of business units, attempts to significantly improve innovation, and cultural change. Examining close to 100 cases, I found that most people did not handle large-scale change well, that they made predictable mistakes, and that they made these mistakes mostly because they had little exposure to highly successful transformations. In a world of increasing turbulence, including unpredictable and terrifying change, the consequences of these errors are very disturbing. The book exposed people to successful change and described an eight-step process used by winning enterprises.

Leading Change was a relatively short 200 pages both because I think that short and to the point is good and because that's all I had to say at the time. Many interesting questions were left unanswered, especially about how people more specifically achieved what was described in that book. These questions were very much on my mind when I received an invitation from Deloitte Consulting to work on a follow-up project. They offered to do massive interviewing to get at the next set of key issues and to collect stories that could help people more deeply understand the eight-step formula. That sounded good to me. I accepted, and the product of the collaboration is this book.

The Deloitte team, headed by Dan Cohen, interviewed over 200 people in more than ninety U.S., European, Australian, and South African organizations. Some of the interviewees were recontacted three or four times as we probed for more and more information. We eventually focused on eighty stories, all of which were cleared with their providers for accuracy. The most instructive thirty-four of those stories are included in this book.

Leading Change describes the eight steps people follow to produce new ways of operating. In *The Heart of Change,* we dig into the core problem people face in all of those steps, and how to successfully deal with that problem. Our main finding, put simply, is that the central issue is never strategy, structure, culture, or systems. All those elements, and others, are important. But the core of the matter is always about changing the behavior of people, and behavior change happens in highly successful situations mostly by speaking to people's feelings. This is true even in organizations that are very focused on analysis and quantitative measurement, even among people who think of themselves as smart in an M.B.A. sense. In highly successful change efforts, people find ways to help others see the problems or solutions in ways that influence emotions, not just thought. Feelings then alter behavior sufficiently to overcome all the many barriers to sensible large-scale change. Conversely, in less successful cases, this seeing-feeling-changing pattern is found less often, if at all.

During my lifetime, the emphasis in books and formal educational settings has been overwhelmingly geared toward analysis and thought. Feelings were seen as "soft" and talked about in a very fuzzy manner. More often than not, emotions were seen as a distraction (hence, "Don't be so emotional!"). Although very recently this has begun to change, I can't remember a time when I heard a concrete, nonmystical discussion of the sort written here about how change leaders used gloves, videocameras, airplanes, office design, new employee orientation, stories, and screen savers to influence feelings and change behavior.

We have structured the book around the eight steps because this is how people experience the process. There is a flow in a successful change effort, and the chapters follow that flow. Throughout, we have tried to employ the book's basic insight as much as possible. Yes, we analyze, but we show the issues with real-life stories told from the point of view of real people. And these people are named—real names except in a few disguised cases.

JOHN KOTTER
Cambridge, Massachusetts

ACKNOWLEDGMENTS

A number of individuals were instrumental in making this book a reality. Our sincere thanks to Isla Beaumont and Richard Skippon for the many hours spent helping us identify companies, conduct interviews, write stories, and think about the implications of those stories. Dustyn Bunker, Stefan Lauber, Judy Le, and Ken Love also helped with the interviews and stories—our hats off to all of them.

Special thanks must go to Deloitte Consulting's Doug McCracken, Stephen Sprinkle, Susan Gretchko, and Gerry Pulvermacher who gave their unyielding time and support to complete the project. A number of Deloitte Consulting principals took the time to assist us in securing interviews. These individuals include John Fox, Doug Lattner, Dave Fornari, John McCue, Andy Konigsberg, Lee Dittmar, Rick Greene, Todd Laviere, Jim MacLachlan, Pete Giulioni, Deon Crafford, Mike McFaul, Mitch Shack, Tom Captain, Jim Bragg, Mike McLaughlin, Jim Haines, Dan Gruber, Jack Ringquist, Brian Lee, Steve Dmetruk, Derek Brown, Gary Coleman, John Flynn, John Harrison, John Reeve, Mark Gardner, Leon Darga, Willie Beshire, Tom Van der Geest, Peter Gertler, Kevin Gromley, Don Decamara, Carol Lindstrom,

Ed Eshbach, Gary Cunningham, Rich Sterbanz, Christina Dorfhuber, Tom Maloney, Marlees Van der Starre, Tricia Bay, Steve Baldwin, Randy Martin, Andrew Gallow, Tony Gerth, Mike Goldberg, Mike LaPorta, and Chris Hooper.

Nancy Dearman, Spencer Johnson, and Jeff Kehoe provided a very special sort of help with the manuscript itself. In addition, dozens of people were kind enough to review drafts of the book. Our thanks to all.

JOHN KOTTER
DAN COHEN

The Heart of Change

THE SINGLE MOST IMPORTANT message in this book is very simple. People change what they do less because they are given *analysis* that shifts their *thinking* than because they are *shown* a truth that influences their *feelings*. This is especially so in large-scale organizational change, where you are dealing with new technologies, mergers and acquisitions, restructurings, new strategies, cultural transformation, globalization, and e-business— whether in an entire organization, an office, a department, or a work group. In an age of turbulence, when you handle this reality well, you win. Handle it poorly, and it can drive you crazy, cost a great deal of money, and cause a lot of pain.

The lessons here come from two sets of interviews, the first completed seven years ago, the second within the last two years. About 400 people from 130 organizations answered our questions. We found, in brief, that

- Highly successful organizations know how to overcome antibodies that reject anything new. They know how to grab opportunities and avoid hazards. They see that *bigger leaps* are increasingly associated with winning big. They see that continuous gradual improvement, by itself, is no longer enough.

- Successful large-scale change is a complex affair that happens in *eight stages*. The flow is this: push urgency up, put together a guiding team, create the vision and strategies, effectively communicate the vision and strategies, remove barriers to action, accomplish short-term wins, keep pushing for wave after wave of change until the work is done, and, finally, create a new culture to make new behavior stick.

- The central challenge in all eight stages is *changing people's behavior*. The central challenge is not strategy, not systems, not culture. These elements and many others can be very important, but the core problem without question is behavior—what people do, and the need for significant shifts in what people do.

- Changing behavior is less a matter of giving people analysis to influence their thoughts than helping them to see a truth *to influence their feelings*. Both thinking and feeling are essential, and both are found in successful organizations, but the heart of change is in the emotions. The flow of see-feel-change is more powerful than that of analysis-think-change.

These distinctions between seeing and analyzing, between feeling and thinking, are critical because, for the most part, we use the latter much more frequently, competently, and comfortably than the former.

When we are frustrated, we sometimes try to convince ourselves there is a decreasing need for large-scale change. But powerful and unceasing forces are driving the turbulence. When frustrated, we sometimes think that problems are inevitable and out of our control. Yet some people handle large-scale change remarkably well. We can all learn from these people. CEOs can learn. First-line supervisors can learn. Nearly anyone caught up in a big change can learn. That's the point of this book.

The Eight Stages of Successful Large-Scale Change

To understand why some organizations are leaping into the future more successfully than others, you need first to see the flow of effective large-scale change efforts. In almost all cases, there is a flow, a set of eight steps that few people handle well.

Step 1

Whether at the top of a large private enterprise or in small groups at the bottom of a nonprofit, those who are most successful at significant change begin their work by creating a sense of *urgency* among relevant people. In smaller organizations, the "relevant" are more likely to number 100 than 5, in larger organizations 1,000 rather than 50. The less successful change leaders aim at 5 or 50 or 0, allowing what is common nearly everywhere—too much complacency, fear, or anger, all three of which can undermine change. A sense of urgency, sometimes developed by very creative means, gets people off the couch, out of a bunker, and ready to move.

Step 2

With urgency turned up, the more successful change agents pull together a *guiding team* with the credibility, skills, connections, reputations, and formal authority required to provide change leadership. This group learns to operate as do all good teams, with trust and emotional commitment. The less successful rely on a single person or no one, weak task forces and committees, or complex governance structures, all without the stature and skills and power to do the job. The landscape is littered with task forces ill equipped to produce needed change.

Step 3

In the best cases, the guiding team creates sensible, clear, simple, uplifting *visions* and sets of strategies. In the less successful cases, there are only detailed plans and budgets that, although necessary, are insufficient, or a vision that is not very sensible in light of what is happening in the world and in the enterprise, or a vision that is created by others and largely ignored by the guiding team. In unsuccessful cases, strategies are often too slow and cautious for a faster-moving world.

Step 4

Communication of the vision and strategies comes next—simple, heartfelt messages sent through many unclogged channels. The goal is to induce understanding, develop a gut-level commitment, and liberate more energy from a critical mass of people. Here, deeds are often more important than words. Symbols speak loudly. Repetition is key. In the less successful cases, there is too little effective communication, or people hear words but don't accept them. Remarkably, smart people undercommunicate or poorly communicate all the time without recognizing their error.

Step 5

In the best situations, you find a heavy dose of *empowerment*. Key obstacles that stop people from acting on the vision are removed. Change leaders focus on bosses who disempower, on inadequate information and information systems, and on self-confidence barriers in people's minds. The issue here is removing obstacles, not "giving power." You can't hand out power in a bag. In less successful situations, people are often left to fend for themselves despite impediments all around. So frustration grows, and change is undermined.

Step 6

With empowered people working on the vision, in cases of great success those people are helped to produce *short-term wins*. The wins are critical. They provide credibility, resources, and momentum to the overall effort. In other cases, the wins come more slowly, less visibly, speak less to what people value, and have more ambiguity as to whether they really are successes. Without a well-managed process, careful selection of initial projects, and fast enough successes, the cynics and skeptics can sink any effort.

Step 7

In the best cases, change leaders *don't let up*. Momentum builds after the first wins. Early changes are consolidated. People shrewdly choose what to tackle next, then create wave after wave of change until the vision is a reality. In less successful cases, people try to do too much at once. They unwittingly quit too soon. They let momentum slip to the point where they find themselves hopelessly bogged down.

Step 8

Finally, in the best cases, change leaders throughout organizations *make change stick* by nurturing a new culture. A new culture—

group norms of behavior and shared values—develops through consistency of successful action over a sufficient period of time. Here, appropriate promotions, skillful new employee orientation, and events that engage the emotions can make a big difference. In other cases, changes float fragile on the surface. A great deal of work can be blown away by the winds of tradition in a remarkably short period of time.

The Flow of Change

The process of change involves subtle points regarding overlapping stages, guiding teams at multiple levels in the organization, handling multiple cycles of change, and more. Because the world is complex, some cases do not rigidly follow the eight-step flow. But the eight steps are the basic pattern associated with significant useful change—all possible *despite* an inherent organizational inclination not to leap successfully into a better future.

Evidence overwhelmingly suggests that the most fundamental problem in all of the stages is changing the behavior of people. The core issue in step 1 is not urgency in some abstract sense. The core issue is the behavior of people who are ignoring how the world is changing, who are frozen in terror by the problems they see, or who do little but bitterly complain. In step 2, the issue is the behavior of those in a position to guide change—especially regarding trust and commitment. In step 3, the core challenge is for people to start acting in a way that will create sensible visions and strategies. For people who know how to plan but have never devised a winning change vision, this behavior change is very big. In step 4, the issue is getting sufficient people to buy into the vision via communication. In step 5, it's acting on that communication—which for some employees will mean doing their jobs in radically new ways. And so on throughout the process.

The Eight Steps for Successful Large-Scale Change

Step	Action	New Behavior
1	Increase urgency	People start telling each other, "Let's go, we need to change things!"
2	Build the guiding team	A group powerful enough to guide a big change is formed and they start to work together well.
3	Get the vision right	The guiding team develops the right vision and strategy for the change effort.
4	Communicate for buy-in	People begin to buy into the change, and this shows in their behavior.
5	Empower action	More people feel able to act, and do act, on the vision.
6	Create short-term wins	Momentum builds as people try to fulfill the vision, while fewer and fewer resist change.
7	Don't let up	People make wave after wave of changes until the vision is fulfilled.
8	Make change stick	New and winning behavior continues despite the pull of tradition, turnover of change leaders, etc.

See, Feel, Change

Significantly changing the behavior of a single person can be exceptionally difficult work. Changing 101 or 10,001 people can be a Herculean task. Yet organizations that are leaping into the future succeed at doing just that. Look carefully at how they act and you'll find another pattern. They succeed, regardless of the stage in the overall process, because their most central activity does not center on formal data gathering, analysis, report writing, and presentations—the sorts of actions typically aimed at changing thinking in order to change behavior. Instead, they compellingly *show* people what the problems are and how to resolve the problems. They provoke responses that reduce feelings that slow and stifle needed change, and they enhance feelings that motivate useful action. The emotional reaction then provides the energy that propels people to push along the change process, no matter how great the difficulties.

The stories presented throughout the book clarify this pattern, showing what can be done to enable the process. In chapter 1 (which deals with urgency), a procurement manager starts a needed change by creating a dramatic presentation. On the boardroom table he piles 424 different kinds of gloves that the firm is currently buying for its workers at dozens of different prices for the same glove and from dozens of different suppliers. First people are shocked, then the gut-level sense of complacency shrinks and urgency grows. It's not just a matter of the data saying that changes are necessary in the purchasing process so people alter their behavior. Instead, it's subtler and deeper. It's a loud sound that catches attention in a day filled with thousands of words and dozens of events. It's an image, hard to shake, that evokes a feeling that we must *do* something.

In chapter 2 (guiding team), the army officer doesn't pull together his new change team with a rational argument. Instead, he shocks them by taking a risk for the greater good with his comments in a meeting. He then helps them begin to tell emotion-packed stories around a campfire. More positive feelings and trust grow, making them act as an effective team.

The aircraft plant manager in chapter 3 (vision and strategies) ceases to just talk to his people about developing ambitious strategies to fit an ambitious quality vision. Instead, he takes dramatic action. He stops the normal production process—just stops it—so everyone must stare all day long at a gigantic plane that can no longer move along the production line. At the same time, he expresses a rock-solid belief that they can find a way to improve quality without delaying delivery. After the initial shock, and with his continuously upbeat behavior, employees begin developing all sorts of new strategies for leaping ahead in procurement, logistics, and quality control.

In chapter 4 (communication), people logically explain why maintaining a lush executive floor is cost-effective in an age of cutbacks—the logic being that it would cost more to change the architecture and décor to make it look less excessive. But that communication convinces few employees and allows cynicism to grow. So they "nuke" the floor, making it less regal, and shock employees in a way that increases their faith in top management and their belief in the vision.

In chapter 5 (empowerment), managers refuse to demote, fire, or "retrain" someone who is staunchly against change and who disempowers others from helping with change. Instead they loan him to a customer, where he is dramatically confronted each day with the problems the customer is having with his products. What he sees generates shock, then feelings that help the man rise to the occasion. He returns to his employer a manager reborn. Approaching his job in a whole new way, he helps the firm make changes that benefit customers, employees, and owners.

In chapter 6 (short-term wins), a manager does not ignore an influential state Senator or sell him on a change effort's progress with graphs and charts. Instead, the manager finds out what the Senator really cares about. Then he dramatically reduces the number of ridiculous, bureaucratic forms needed to be filled out in that area. He shows the Senator the result, surprising the man in the most positive sense. As a result, the Senator begins actively supporting the change effort.

In chapter 7 (not letting up), a task force knows top management behavior is slowing down the change process. But instead of ducking the issue, or trying to describe it in antiseptic terms, the task force creates a hilarious video with actors spoofing the problem. The amusing, nonconfrontational video gives those executives trying to create change a much-needed tool for legitimizing new top management behavior.

In chapter 8 (making change stick), staff write a good speech about the values the firm has created and needs to strengthen and retain if their transformation is to be firmly entrenched. But the real power comes when they present a real customer to employees. He tells an inspirational story showing the consequences of living those values.

Stories like these reveal a core pattern associated with successful change.

1. **SEE.** People find a problem in some stage of the change process—too many of their colleagues are behaving complacently, no one is developing a sensible strategy, too many are letting up before the strategy has been achieved. They then create dramatic, eye-catching, compelling situations that help others visualize the problem or a solution to the problem.

2. **FEEL.** The visualizations awaken feelings that facilitate useful change or ease feelings that are getting in the way. Urgency, optimism, or faith may go up. Anger, complacency, cynicism, or fear may go down.

3. **CHANGE.** The new feelings change or reinforce new behavior, sometimes very different behavior. People act much less complacently. They try much harder to make a good vision a reality. They don't stop before the work is done, even if the road seems long.

Achieving a Change of Behavior
within Each of the Eight Steps

Almost Always the Core Method Is: SEE-FEEL-CHANGE	Rarely the Core Method Is: ANALYSIS-THINK-CHANGE
1. HELP PEOPLE SEE. Compelling, eye-catching, dramatic situations are created to help others visualize problems, solutions, or progress in solving complacency, strategy, empowerment, or other key problems within the eight steps. *As a result*	**1. GIVE PEOPLE ANALYSIS.** Information is gathered and analyzed, reports are written, and presentations are made about problems, solutions, or progress in solving urgency, teamwork, communication, momentum slippage, or other key problems within the eight steps. *As a result*
2. SEEING SOMETHING NEW HITS THE EMOTIONS. The visualizations provide useful ideas that hit people at a deeper level than surface thinking. They evoke a visceral response that reduces emotions that block change and enhances those that support it.	**2. DATA AND ANALYSIS INFLUENCE HOW WE THINK.** The information and analysis change people's thinking. Ideas inconsistent with the needed change are dropped or modified.
3. EMOTIONALLY CHARGED IDEAS CHANGE BEHAVIOR OR REINFORCE CHANGED BEHAVIOR.	**3. NEW THOUGHTS CHANGE BEHAVIOR OR REINFORCE CHANGED BEHAVIOR.**

Successful see-feel-change tactics tend to be clever, not clumsy, and never cynically manipulative. They often have an afterglow, where the story of the event is told again and again or where there is a remaining visible sign of the event that influences additional people over time. When done well over all eight stages of a change process, the results can be breathtaking. Mature (old-fashioned, clunky, or heavy) organizations take a leap into the future. Laggards start to become leaders. Leaders jump farther ahead.

The point is not that careful data gathering, analysis, and presentation are unimportant. They are important. Sometimes it is behavior changed by analysis that sends people into a see-feel-change process. Sometimes change launched through feelings creates a radically better approach to analysis. Often small changes are a necessary part of a larger change effort, and the small changes are driven by analysis. Occasionally, careful analysis is required to get show-me-the-numbers finance people or engineers in the mood to see.

But analysis has at least three major limitations. First, in a remarkable number of cases, you don't need it to find the big truths. You may not need to do much work to find that the old strategy isn't working and that a new one isn't being embraced. You don't need a fifty-page report to see there is insufficient new product development and that a number of factors make it impossible for the engineers to do what is necessary. You don't need reams of financial data to learn that you cannot stay out of e-business and that the first step is simply to take the first step. It isn't necessary for a team of psychologists to study Fred and his team to find out they are failing and must be replaced. Yes, there are many exceptions—deciding on which $100 million IT system to buy, for example—but the general point is valid.

Second, analytical tools have their limitations in a turbulent world. These tools work best when parameters are known, assumptions are minimal, and the future is not fuzzy.

Third, good analysis rarely motivates people in a big way. It changes thought, but how often does it send people running out the door to act in significantly new ways? And motivation is not a thinking word; it's a feeling word.

We fail at change efforts not because we are stupid, overcontrolled, and unemotional beings, although it can seem that way at times. We fail because we haven't sufficiently experienced highly successful change. Without that experience, we are too often left pessimistic, fearful, or without enough faith to act. So we not only behave in less effective ways, we don't even try.

Consider the implications of this pattern in an age of accelerating change, at a time when we are making a mind-boggling transition from an industrial to an information/knowledge economy. Consider the implications in light of how managers, management educators, and others today deal with large-scale change.

Of course there are many difficulties here, but being uninformed and pessimistic does not help. We need more leaps into the future. And although we are becoming better at this, there is no reason that we cannot learn to become much better still.

In light of the stakes, we must become better still.

Using the Book

Because they help *show,* the stories in the book are very important. As a reader, glancing at the figures, reading a bit of the text, and moving on does not work especially well. If you are in a rush and want to learn from the book quickly, read three or four stories and look at the end-of-chapter figures. You might choose the stories in whichever chapter seems of most relevance. Or you might go to "Gloves on the Boardroom Table" in the step 1 chapter, "The Plane Will Not Move!" in the step 3 chapter, and "Retooling the Boss" in the step 5 chapter.

No matter how you read the book, feel free to copy a story and send it to your colleagues. The more a relevant story circulates among your colleagues, and the more it creates useful dialogue, the better.

In a recent edition of *Fortune* magazine, Jack Welch is quoted as saying, "You've got to talk about change every second of the day." That's a bit of an extreme position, but maybe extreme is what wins.

STEP ONE
Increase Urgency

STEP TWO
Build the Guiding Team

STEP THREE
Get the Vision Right

STEP FOUR
Communicate for Buy-In

STEP FIVE
Empower Action

STEP SIX
Create Short-Term Wins

STEP SEVEN
Don't Let Up

STEP EIGHT
Make Change Stick

STEP 1

Increase Urgency

I N SUCCESSFUL CHANGE EFFORTS, THE first step is making sure sufficient people act with sufficient urgency—with on-your-toes behavior that looks for opportunities and problems, that energizes colleagues, that beams a sense of "let's go." Without enough urgency, large-scale change can become an exercise in pushing a gigantic boulder up a very tall mountain.

Off to a Bad Start

Have you ever seen a variation on this story?

Getting the Bosses' Approval

From Ted Watson

The general idea—hardly unique to us—was to do business consistently across all of our operating units. We would have the same approach to conducting any activity regardless of whether a manager worked in Birmingham or Buffalo. We would use the same basic steps to purchase a pen, generator, or a hammer. The point was to use new technology to take advantage of economies of scale.

The executive committee for our company met one month to discuss changes that were needed in our package system. Before that session, articles had been sent to the execs about the good and the bad aspects of the existing systems. A small team of people had focused carefully on the economic analysis, looking closely at our current software programs, in particular. At the meeting, they presented their case. "The problem we have is this. Technology offers us an opportunity . . . ." Charts, graphs, and flowcharts spelled this out clearly. The executive team listened.

There were questions at the meeting. "How long will this take?" "Who else has used this software?" "How well has the software worked for others?" But there was little controversy and not much discussion. These conversations, the offline talks before the big meeting, the CEO's backing, and the meeting itself seemed to produce agreement.

So we started implementation. Within a few months, the number of phone calls I received from people in the divisions began to grow exponentially. People would say, "How long is this going to take? In *my* business we can't . . . ." "The cost versus benefit for *our* business unit is no good. Why do we . . . ?" "The disruption is going to be unacceptable to *us* because of the people you put on the transformation team." I tried to explain the business case. But I could have spent entire days on the telephone listening to all this.

Basically, each division had many people who wanted to continue to run their business the way they had always run it. They would accept new software as long as they suffered little inconvenience and little change except reduced costs. They wanted their financial reporting to have their traditional look and feel. They wanted to do maintenance scheduling their way and not the way it was being suggested. They said their emergency call-out process just needed a minor tune-up, or that they had always required five signatures to approve a purchase and they had to keep it that way to run their business. It went on and on and on and on. My attention was being diverted to dealing with the avalanche of calls, concerns, and issues.

To make a long story short, we hit a wall. We had to stop, go back, and start over. It was tough work, the second time around.

Four sets of behaviors commonly stop the launch of needed change. The first is complacency, driven by false pride or arrogance. A second is immobilization, self-protection, a sort of hiding in the closet, driven by fear or panic. Another is you-can't-make-me-move deviance, driven by anger. The last is a very pessimistic attitude that leads to constant hesitation. Whatever the reason, the consequences are similar. People do not look carefully at the evidence, get on their toes, and start moving. Instead, they hold back or complain if others initiate new action, with the result that a needed change effort doesn't start or doesn't start well.

In "Bosses' Approval," the implicit assumption underlying the approach was that these behaviors, and the feelings behind them, either weren't there or wouldn't be that relevant once the management committee said yes. These are huge assumptions, and, as it turned out in "Approval," very poor assumptions. At multiple levels in that organization, there were large pockets of complacency—"We have many challenges; uniform business processes is a very low priority." There was fear—"Can I handle this project and still make plan?" There was anger—"Why are they shoving this 'uniform' nonsense down my throat?" There was pessimism—"We'll waste a fortune on this software and it will never work well." There was cynicism—"I wonder how much commission the slick guy who sold us the system made?" Those leading the change inevitably hit this sturdy wall.

Off to a Good Start

Here is a second case with a completely different approach, based on a completely different set of assumptions.

The Videotape of the Angry Customer

From Tim Wallace

One night I was having dinner with one of our largest customers to thank him for the business he gave us. We were talking about one of our core products and he said that he had to make alterations in the product after receiving a shipment. Since this was a built-to-order item, that was ridiculous. The alterations cost him money and wasted time. Naturally, he was not a bit happy about that.

I told him that I was *very* sorry and that we'd have a group of our people address the issues as soon as possible. He looked unimpressed even though I think it was obvious I was being sincere. "It's not as if I have never told your employees about this," he said, "but they don't listen to what we say." He explained that when he identified needed changes in the product or how it was made, our people would do what he asked, but then when he returned in a few weeks the problem had reemerged. "We ask again and again for things to be changed and the person we talk to nods his head but he doesn't seem to listen."

It occurred to me that probably only a few of our people had ever heard from this man directly, and even they may have never seen him as frustrated as he was over that dinner. So I asked him if I could send one of our staff around the next day with a videocamera to record what he was saying. I'm sure he was taken aback, but I told him I was serious and that I thought this could help us both. We talked some more, and with a little bit of selling he agreed.

A few of my people went to see him the next day with a video-cam. They asked him to be totally candid, to hold nothing back. For the most part he did. They shot thirty minutes in one take, and with a little editing, the video came out to be fifteen minutes.

Back at the plant, we put about fifty people in a meeting room. Someone turned on the TV, and there was the unhappy customer.

Their response was fascinating. Most people seem to have been genuinely surprised. They hadn't spent much time with customers and they had probably never heard this type of strong, negative feedback. I suspect a few people wondered whether this was an odd case, but their eyes were glued to the TV. A few mouths actually dropped open. Of course, some people thought the customer was wrong. "He doesn't understand." "He needs to be educated." "The reason why. . . ." But they were in the minority.

After the video, we had a discussion of how to fix the problems and keep them fixed so we would have a satisfied customer. People started throwing out ideas. As you can imagine, some of the ideas weren't very practical. Nevertheless, it was a good discussion.

We showed the video to about 400 employees in total. Again, a minority was defensive. But just as many were saying, "We've got to do something about this. We've got to do something." I think even

the ones on the fence were afterward more likely to listen to any customers that we brought into the plant.

We did more videotaping. It cost virtually nothing. This wasn't
meant to solve all our problems, but it helped chip away at a serious
barrier to improvement. This plant came to us through a company
we acquired. That company had been a leader in its industry for a
long time. The employees probably thought they had all the answers.
They were the experts, skilled craftsmen. But they were also anything
but customer focused. It was probably "Sure, fine, now get out of
the way so I can do my job, which I understand and you don't. I'm
the professional here; you're an annoyance." With this attitude, it's
hard to get off the dime and better satisfy your customer's needs.

Getting off the dime is the central challenge in step 1.

The histories leading up to this story and to "Bosses' Approval"
share many common elements. Both organizations had experienced a considerable amount of success over the years. Both faced
more competition and cost pressures. Both needed to change to
meet the challenges of the twenty-first century. But look how
radically different the stories are.

In "Approval," the focus was mostly on getting the management committee to say yes, and the method mostly one of analysis to influence thinking. In "Videotape," the focus was on a lack
of urgency among the factory workers (and probably the management too). The method was to show them a video to influence
their feelings. The video gave them:

- very concrete, visual information (not intangible data
  points such as "7.2 percent of our customers . . .")

- a dramatic offering (not a dull speech about customer
  orientation)

The Videotape of the Angry Customer

Seeing

Employees see a videotape of an angry yet important customer. The person showing the tape to employees has credibility, and he doesn't serve it up in an angry way (no "Would you dummies look at this!").

Feeling

Most employees are surprised. Some become fearful or mad. Many find false pride dropping a notch and a sense of urgency growing within them—"We gotta do something."

Changing

Some people start acting defensively and cling to the status quo. More begin (tentatively) looking for problems, listening to customers, listening to management when they talk about the need for change. In an organization of "craftsmen" who think they are the experts and they alone know what's right, this is a big shift in behavior.

- a real problem from the point of view of the customer (not a manager's "opinion")

- information that hit the emotions ("What?" "Wow!")

- the emotions of large numbers of people (not just the bosses)

- an opportunity to reduce their feelings of false pride without the intervention of an angry or threatening manager (no "You idiots!")

The result was that pessimism, fear, and anger did not increase among most employees, but urgency did increase, and a change effort was better positioned for launch. The key was the video—probably of medium quality and shot with inexpensive equipment, so that's not where the power lay. The power started with the credibility of a real customer and his honest comments. But "customer data" could have been offered in a two-page memo. The video worked because it was much more compelling. Video plays better to our brains, hard-wired from thousands of years of evolution to absorb deeply what we see, in particular, but also what we hear and touch. The eyes pull in gobs of information every second. If you doubt this, look at the size of a one-minute video file in your computer compared with a text file that you might read in one minute. And visual information does not get dumped into some front-of-the-brain processor. It quickly goes deeper.

The video was presented in a safe context. There were no screams of "If we don't fix this, the company will go down the tubes," "Who's responsible for this mess?" or "Here's what we have to do and you *will* do it starting tomorrow." So fear and anger did not escalate. The tone of the presentation may have actually reduced both.

In "Bosses' Approval," the sell-the-case approach probably did increase anger by shoving a project down the throats of division managers. It probably did increase fear in people who had no idea about the effects of a complex new technology. It certainly did little to reduce those feelings that support complacent behavior. None of this helped increase urgency.

Making a business case and receiving top management approval are obviously not inherently bad. But when we find these actions at the beginning of successful change efforts, they are a part of a larger activity aimed at helping to lower feelings undermining urgency. Data and thinking are obviously not inherently unhelpful. But when you find them at the beginning of successful large-scale change, they are aimed at supporting a more powerful method —one based on helping people to see a truth, feel differently, and then act with more urgency.

Developing a Change "Vision" First

One reason people start a change process with the creation and presentation of a recommendation is because they want clarity of direction. How can you begin without knowing where you are going? With little if any sense of direction at the start, doesn't change risk moving the wrong way?

A similar logic leads people to begin change with the creation of a vision. Shape the vision; make it a reality. It's easy to find successful cases where step 1 seems to be the emergence of a leader with a vision, or a leader who works with others to create the vision.

Here is one example of what can happen when you start with creating a vision. The specifics are related to short-term crises, but the same sort of result is common no matter what the context.

When Alligators Are Nipping at Your Heels

From Nick Pearce

We needed to radically change the organization if we were to be an important part of the future. Because we had problems that were very visible, crisis-like problems, I assumed we did not have to spend much time trying to get people's attention. So I spent all of my time in the first two or three months trying to facilitate a discussion among the executive team. We talked in big-picture terms. What are the key transformation issues? What might a good vision be? I worked very hard at this.

It became difficult to get our senior team together to talk. I would have to repeatedly chase them to make sure they would come to the meetings, even after calling them to "confirm" that the meeting was still on. If I learned that someone was not going to be there, I'd look into that and see if I could turn it around. Then, even after herding them into a room, someone would inevitably say, "Sorry, but I've got an important meeting starting in an hour so I'll have to duck out of this session early." This was not helped by the fact that I was not their boss.

Without any enthusiasm, without the attendance, the end result wasn't very good. We did manage to put a vision, of sorts, on paper. But it was only a paper exercise. Our executive's attention was elsewhere. I'd give myself a 10 out of 10 for effort, and a 0 out of 10 for results.

I did not realize at the time how massive our short-term problems were. There were new contracts that needed to be negotiated and understood. There were maintenance and operational schedules that had to be planned out using different suppliers and budgetary processes. There were the new systems that people needed to start working with or we couldn't plan the service effectively. At one point we were planning this only three weeks in advance. Normally it would have been months ahead. When you added it all up, it was frightening. If you had major responsibilities, I'm sure it felt as if the house was burning down around you.

So I shifted my entire focus. Instead of saying "Let's spend Friday working on the vision statement," I'd say, "Our maintenance program is disintegrating around our ears so let's do something about it." This tactic got the senior team's attention and started to make a difference. But then, while putting out the fires, we encouraged a discussion of what we needed to do in the future to avoid the problems we had. So while we were dealing with what we needed to spend money on to get this sorted out, and sorted out *now,* we also talked a bit about how we would need to structure the investment program in the future. This helped to build the basis for wanting to go on to the really big issues. This started to build interest in, and urgency for, the bigger transformation problems. We should have done more of this from the start.

I now believe that you can't, and shouldn't, worry about vision and long-term transformation when the house is burning down. When you are committed to helping your bosses rebuild the organization, and you see all the change that is going on around you, and you see the probable magnitude of the required transformation, you want to get on with it. Even if you acknowledge the size of the immediate crisis, you want to use the crisis only to get people's attention and then to run ahead to vision. In our case, this did not work well in making people want to deal with the bigger issues. Not at all.

When alligators are nipping at your heels, you need to deal with the alligators. To some degree at least, I think you have to get the crises under control. You have to focus on putting out the big fires and on anything that can quickly restart those fires. Otherwise, there will be no energy for a bigger transformation, and, worse case, you will get into such trouble that you will never be able to build a strong organization.

A CEO, not ours, once took over an ailing business and said, "The last thing we need now is a vision." I didn't understand his point. I do now.

The CEO was probably Lou Gerstner after he took over IBM. At the time, many people didn't see his point. What IBM needed, as in "Alligators," was first to stop the bleeding, then to generate some minimum urgency for the bigger task. Vision was not the issue yet—not even close. Gerstner may have had the beginnings of a vision in his own mind. But that was not the key organizational challenge, and refining the vision was not where he spent his time.

The more general issue is jumping ahead. People do this all the time, especially to stage 3, the vision step. They do so in situations with short-term crises, like that in "Alligators," and in situations with no crises at all. Jumping to vision, or perhaps even more often to strategy, is tempting because it seems so logical. Obviously, you cannot have sensible change without sensible direction. So setting direction must come first. Then you implement it with some variation of "change management."

The problem with this logic is that really good change visions and strategies are increasingly difficult to create. The world is complex and turbulence is growing. Even the issues facing a small company or a small department in a much larger organization can be very complicated. The idea of one hero who figures it all out himself is increasingly a myth. A team is needed that has the right people, a commitment to the hard task, and the capacity to work together well. Creating that team (step 2) has to happen before you work on vision (step 3). Finding the right people and gaining commitment to a hard task and to each other is greatly facilitated by a sense of urgency (step 1).

There is one exception. If urgency is already high and the right team is already in place, then, in a sense, step 1 in the process is vision. But much too often, change initiators misjudge how much urgency exists for a large-scale transformation. "Our people know we need a big change and they're ready to go," the change leader tells us. "Oh, not everyone, but enough." Talk to people in his organization, including some who are needed to create the vision, and you find that many think there already has been too much change. You find that some believe a few more quick fixes will do the job, others say they are far too busy to take on more challenges, and still others think what they do works just fine, thank you. Vision-first advocates also sometimes misjudge the change team that's in place. They don't see that the group was great for the past, not the future, or that the group does not work well enough together to guide a major change.

To repeat: If you have sufficient urgency and a good enough team, step 1, in a sense, is vision. But how often do you think that is the case?

Crises, Burning Platforms, and Fear

"Alligators" suggests another important lesson—this one about crises and fear.

Because moving a mountain of an enterprise can be so hard, you might logically think that a crisis, externally forced or internally induced, is necessary. Forget trying to persuade them; light their pants on fire.

There is some truth here. You could argue that in "The Videotape of the Angry Customer," the key player created a sort of mini-crisis. But more often than not, when we speak of crises, we mean "burning platforms" that force people to jump away from their comfortable positions. Burning platforms can work. But they can also create a panic that stops new action. Sometimes we think that fear is good for people, making them less complacent. This can be true. But in large-scale change, if fear is not converted to a positive urgency, and with some speed, it can become a significant liability, not an asset. With too much fear, some people will focus on the immediate source of anxiety, nothing else, as in "Alligators." Some will find fire extinguishers, put out the flames, and then climb back on the platform. Some will freeze, hide, or become very self-protective. People can start to think, "Who cares about the organization? I don't want to die."

This is a very important point. Fear can produce movement. It can dynamite a cement wall. But we have yet to see great transformations launched with fear as the primary and *sustaining* force. Urgency sustains change. When we are frustrated and mad at a group of people, fear can sound like a great idea. But it never seems to take you successfully through steps 2 to 8 because people eventually focus on self-preservation instead of organizational transformation. When 50 or 50,000 people have self-preservation as their number one goal, what happens when you try to build a guiding team that works together seamlessly? What happens when you ask departments to creatively coordinate their actions? What happens if Fred can only do his critical job if Helen makes behind-the-scene sacrifices?

But I'm Just a Munchkin

We sometimes understand these points about fear, anger, complacency, urgency, and crises, yet do little to help start a change effort because we feel powerless to do so. "I'm not the boss. Given all the constraints on my action, what can I do?" Staff can feel this way, middle managers can feel this way, executive vice presidents (really) can feel this way. The I'm-not-powerful-enough sensation can be very strong, very debilitating, and enormously frustrating.

In some situations the constraints and lack of power are overwhelming. Nevertheless, action is often possible.

Here's our favorite step 1 story. As you will see, the key players are far from the CEO.

Gloves on the Boardroom Table

From Jon Stegner

We had a problem with our whole purchasing process. I was convinced that a great deal of money was being wasted and would continue to be wasted into the future, and that we didn't even know how much money was being thrown away. I thought we had an opportunity to drive down purchasing costs not by 2 percent but by something in the order of $1 billion over the next five years. A change this big meant a big shift in the process. This would not be possible, however, unless many people, especially in top management, saw the opportunity, which for the most part they did not. So nothing was happening.

To get a sense of the magnitude of the problem, I asked one of our summer students to do a small study of how much we pay for the different kinds of gloves used in our factories and how many different gloves we buy. I chose one item to keep it simple, something all the plants use and something we can all easily relate to.

When the student completed the project, she reported that our factories were purchasing 424 different kinds of gloves! *Four hundred and twenty four*. Every factory had their own supplier and their own negotiated price. The same glove could cost $5 at one factory and $17 at another. Five dollars or even $17 may not seem like much money, but we buy a *lot* of gloves, and this was just one example of our purchasing problem. When I examined what she had found, even I couldn't believe how bad it was.

The student was able to collect a sample of every one of the 424 gloves. She tagged each one with the price on it and the factory it was used in. Then she sorted the bags by division in the firm and type of glove.

We gathered them all up and put them in our boardroom one day. Then we invited all the division presidents to come visit the room.

What they saw was a large, expensive table, normally clean or with a few papers, now stacked high with gloves. Each of our executives stared at this display for a minute. Then each said something like, "We buy all these different kinds of gloves?" Well, as a matter of fact, yes we do. "Really?" Yes, really. Then they walked around the table. Most, I think, were looking for the gloves that their factories were using. They could see the prices. They looked at two gloves that seemed exactly alike, yet one was marked $3.22 and the other $10.55.

It's a rare event when these people don't have anything to say. But that day, they just stood with their mouths gaping.

This demonstration quickly gained notoriety. The gloves became part of a traveling road show. They went to every division. They went to dozens of plants. Many, many people had the opportunity to look at the stacks of gloves. The road show reinforced at every level of the organization a sense of "this is how bad it is."

Through more research, again done quickly and inexpensively by one of our students, we discovered what some of our competitors were doing. The "competitive benchmarking" was added to the road show. As a result, we were given a mandate for change. People would say "We must act now," which of course we did, and saved a great deal of money that could be used in much more sensible ways.

Even today, people still talk about the glove story.

It's easy to see why they do.

The key players in "Gloves" are not the bosses. One important participant is just a summer student. Yet these not-top-managers helped launch an effort that radically changed the purchasing process in a large organization and saved hundreds of millions of dollars.

Their method was similar to that in "The Videotape of the Angry Customer." Go after the emotions with concrete and almost smellable evidence, not just the abstractions so favored by the rational mind. Use evidence you can see, not just words and numbers. Create a dramatic, look-at-this presentation, yet one based on honest facts and no coercion. As a result—and this is the key point—feelings are touched and changed, yet without provoking a debilitating sense of "I'm going to die" or an angry counterattack. Instead, the sense of urgency goes up and the change effort is launched.

Cheap and Easy

Both "Gloves" and "Videotape" make another important point. Helping to prepare an organization for large-scale change doesn't require a million dollars and six months. Much can be done quickly and inexpensively.

Here's a third example of a cheap and easy action to help with step 1 problems. In this case, instead of videos or gloves, we find portraits.

The CEO Portrait Gallery

From Ron Marshall

When you walked into the lobby of our main headquarters building, there was a receptionist directly in front of you, a small sitting area to her left with chairs, and a coffee table with magazines to keep visitors occupied. Directly opposite the sitting area were ten or so portraits of stern-looking former CEOs. It was a cross between a mini art gallery and a shrine. Every time you walked into the building you passed these pictures. Every time you left the building you passed these pictures. We had every CEO going back to 1885, all the way back into the last century. Formal oil portraits glorified the

CEO and the past. They'd been there for years, looking down with a paternalistic benevolence as people came and went.

The gallery was meant to be a tribute to a great group of people and to show a sense of continuity. But it was also a look backward in an age in which looking backward can get you into trouble. It was a symbol of endless success at a time when we weren't that successful. It was a tribute to the importance of the CEO (and, subtly, to the unimportance of non-CEOs). It suggested an us (CEOs) versus them (everyone else) attitude. And in some ways, it really was a shrine. The only other time I had seen anything like that was when I was at Woolworth. Woolworth is not a great model of a twenty-first-century business.

A couple of my executives said, "Well, when are they putting your picture up?" I said "Never." Shortly after that conversation, I had all the old CEOs removed. We just took them out. In an old firm like ours, this was a shock. Word of this single little action spread faster than any speech that I could have possibly made.

We could have done nothing. We could have put up other sorts of art, or reproductions from a museum. We could have used pictures of the current executive committee. We could have pictures of our facilities or products. Any of these would have made a point. But we didn't do any of that. We replaced the CEOs with pictures of our customer's stores.

These aren't expensive shots from a famous photographer. Just pictures of customer's stores. This too became the talk of the company.

Soon after the new pictures were up, several members on my executive team stopped by my office and told me that it was about time we started to focus on our customers. In the cafeteria, I overheard a conversation between two of our associates. One individual said he really liked the idea of getting rid of those old pictures. "If Ron is really serious about improving customer service we need a fresh outlook and not more of the same old 'we are great' speeches."

It was one little change, but it had its effect. People began paying more attention to our customers and their requirements. Without that, without seeing how their needs were changing and how we weren't meeting those needs well, we were going nowhere.

A colleague of ours, Harvard psychologist Stephen Kosslyn, suggests an interesting alternative in this case, but one that still uses a showing/feeling method. Why not, he asks, put up new sets of pictures, each with three components: a former CEO in the left lower corner looking to the right, a company building at the time of his tenure directly above the CEO, and a typical customer's store in that era to the right of both. Most of the space would still be a picture of a store, but now with a CEO looking at it. With this positioning, a slightly different message is implicit. With CEOs looking at stores, the pictures suggest an even stronger customer focus. With evolving buildings, the pictures suggest an adaptation to change. This approach would still have the power of a strong visual surprise, yet it would create less anger from those with an emotional attachment to the former CEOs and the firm's past.

Obviously, one cheap and easy action is far, far from a silver bullet. In some situations, especially where you are still very successful, videotaping, portrait shifting, and much more may be needed. People are successfully taking those actions even as you read this book. Change leaders are bringing in new people from the outside, people who already have a sense of urgency. Done well, the newcomers' behavior catches attention in a very useful way. Change leaders are finding ways to get their subordinates, colleagues, or bosses to visit other, better firms. The visibly superior practices catch attention. Change leaders are designing yearly management meetings in ways that are a total break from tradition. The fact that senior management at these meetings acts (not just

An Exercise That Might Help

(You can do this exercise by yourself, but it may be better with a few friends.)

1. For the organizational unit over which you have some influence (corporate, division, department), is there a need for large-scale change? Are competitors leaping ahead but your organization is not? Are there technological discontinuities that others are exploiting but your organization is not? Are you bogged down in the past? Are there wonderful new opportunities that will require significant change on your part? If yes,

    • How high is the urgency regarding these problems or opportunities?

    • What behavior, not just words, lead you to this conclusion?

    • What creates or supports this behavior and the underlying feelings? Consider the following possibilities: historical success; systems that poorly measure today's achievements against external referents; lack of customer contact; symbols that are out of touch with today's market reality; visible examples of excess, of throwing money around when others are winning and costs are tight; the internally focused attitudes of bosses; lack of widely shared data on performance versus competitors; too much "happy talk" from the management that is out of touch with the real world; low overall performance standards relative to competitors; a kill-the-messenger or low-candor culture; subunit goals that allow a subunit to look good as the ship is sinking.

2. What can you do that is dramatic, attention grabbing, and memorable to attack the problem of insufficient urgency?

- Can you show people something that is already there, like an unhappy customer?

- Can you create something new that will highlight the problem, as in "Gloves" or "Portrait Gallery"?

- Can you do something indirectly—like showing a boss how much his or her subordinates are creating complacency in their subordinates?

- If you have never done much of anything like this before, can you find a collaborator who has?

- Note: In thinking about these questions, look for cheap and easy opportunities. Remember, you have an organization to run and products or services to be delivered or built today. Be realistic and opportunistic.

3. Watch out!

Remember also that a good analytical report or presentation of your answer to point 1 could, if given to the right people at the right time, make a difference. But if it is not visually compelling, dramatic, attention grabbing, and memorable, it will probably have very limited impact.

---

talks) with a sense of urgency catches attention. Change leaders are bringing in valued customers, with surprising messages, to regular management meetings. Done well, urgency goes up, and a transformation is off to a good start.

Increase Urgency

Raise a feeling of urgency so that people say "let's go," making a change effort well positioned for launch.

WHAT WORKS

- Showing others the need for change with a compelling object that they can actually see, touch, and feel
- Showing people valid and dramatic evidence from outside the organization that demonstrates that change is required
- Looking constantly for cheap and easy ways to reduce complacency
- Never underestimating how much complacency, fear, and anger exists, even in good organizations

WHAT DOES NOT WORK

- Focusing exclusively on building a "rational" business case, getting top management approval, and racing ahead while mostly ignoring all the feelings that are blocking change
- Ignoring a lack of urgency and jumping immediately to creating a vision and strategy
- Believing that without a crisis or burning platform you can go nowhere
- Thinking that you can do little if you're not the head person

STORIES TO REMEMBER

- Getting the Bosses' Approval
- The Videotape of the Angry Customer
- When Alligators are Nipping at Your Heels
- Gloves on the Boardroom Table
- The CEO Portrait Gallery

STEP 2

Build the Guiding Team

A FEELING OF URGENCY HELPS greatly in putting together the right group to guide change and in creating essential teamwork within the group. When there is urgency, more people want to help provide leadership, even if there are personal risks. More people are willing to pull together, even if there are no short-term personal rewards. But additional effort is necessary to get the right people in place with the trust, emotional commitment, and teamwork to do the job. That's the step 2 challenge.

When the Team Is Not a Team

A common step 2 problem is that those who should be driving change are not doing their job, and nobody wants to confront the issue.

The Blues versus the Greens

From Gary Lockhart

Nobody wanted to admit it, and we refused to talk about it, but we were like two gangs, the Blues and the Greens. We didn't fight, because someone said, "I expect you guys to be friendly and nice to each other." The only reason we didn't go after each other was because there were "cops" around.

This all started with the merger. We knew we needed to get our act together in order to create a new company. Doing this well was very important because although the public might think firms like ours are all alike, it's not true. Our two companies had different product offerings, different strengths and weaknesses, different cultures. We needed to settle whether this was going to be more like Company A or more like Company B, and then make it happen.

Nobody wanted to talk about the problem in public, but we knew senior management was not up to the task. A couple of groups went to a well-known institute to think and talk. They read and heard ideas from great books and great people. They filled up paper. It was very civilized. If you'd have walked in and asked if they were now a team, people probably would have said, "Sure. Now we are a team with shared values. See, the values are over there on that flip chart." But it wasn't true.

Not much was worked out at that meeting or afterward because there was too little open, honest communication. When there were things people didn't like, they wouldn't speak up. They would just harbor bad feelings.

You'd have these conversations where someone would say, "I think with the opening in the marketing group, Jerry Johnson is the best man for the job. Jerry has 16 years of experience and excellent reviews. He is very skilled at X and Y and don't forget about Z." That would be someone from the Green team. Of course, Jerry would be a member of the same team. Then someone from the Blue team would say, "Well Jerry sounds excellent, but in this job the number one challenge is going to be such and such, and I would worry that Jerry, terrific person that he is, doesn't have that experience. But Fred Jones does." Fred, of course, is from the Blue team. Then a Green team player says, "You make a good point, but I think if you look closely—and I know Jerry so I can say this with great confidence—he is just the type of person who can learn to handle that challenge in no time at all. He's a very quick take." But at the same time, you could almost hear the conversation going on over a different channel: "You're getting too many of the good jobs. If you don't stop the land grab, we're going to rip the heart out of one of your people." "Oh yeah, you want to fight now? It's seven against five and we've got the seven. You sure you want to do that? Remember, our leader's nickname is The Decapitator." "You guys are going too far. Our Larry is a bad guy and he knows how to use a chain."

No one was willing, or at least no one could figure out a way, to talk about this honestly in public. The merger-related politics were very difficult. We talked around the issues. Meanwhile the business problems were growing.

The firm was not achieving the "synergies" and economies of scale promised in the merger proposal. Worse, it was slowing to 50 miles an hour in a world where slow is a death wish. After a brief boost by the merger announcement, the stock began sinking.

With fragmentation at the top, there was no cohesive force strong enough to drive the difficult, nonincremental change that was needed. Out of frustration, the CEO tried at one point to work around his senior team. But he knew, at least intuitively, that the approach was hopeless. Even an extremely talented person does not have enough time, skills, connections, reputation, leadership capacity, and energy to lead change alone except in small groups. Somebody in the firm, again out of frustration, suggested delegating big pieces of the needed change to task forces. That strategy may have been tried once or twice, and, if so, with little effect. When the CEO can't do it, how can a lower-level task force?

It was about a year later that we hired a respected facilitator to run a management meeting. We had the top 100 or so of us over at a Northwestern University conference facility. For the first time we really started getting at the real issue, which of course was the top team itself.

The facilitator who was trying to take us through this process ended up becoming very frustrated and mad. He picked up that we were being very polite and cautious in what we were saying and that we would not engage in the real issues. So I guess he figured it was hopeless unless we were willing to look at ourselves, and he said so. He's the one that started talking about the split into the Blue and Green teams.

After the facilitator let us have it, the meeting the next day became full of "honest conflict." Once we stopped biting our tongues, the management issues came out in a more forthright fashion than ever before—as a much more open, less politically correct dialogue. People began to let their hair down. "We've been meaning to say this. We've been needing to get it off our chests." I think there was this great relief in letting that out into the open and giving people a chance to respond. If nothing else, we left with a better respect for each other.

From that point, our "leadership team" finally started to become a leadership team. It wasn't a matter of "We had that meeting and now everything is okay." What the meeting did, I think, was allow us to get started. And when the genie is out of the bottle, it's hard to cram it back in. It's been a long road since then in building the new company, but that meeting began a more open dialogue that has helped us build trust and ultimately an actual team.

This company ignored the step 2 challenge at first, then attacked it with an overly intellectualized discussion of "values." In both cases, the underlying feelings creating fragmentation, undermining the formation of a powerful enough guiding group, and blocking progress were largely avoided. This dynamic changed only when someone showed emotionally honest and open behavior, spoke the unspeakable, connected to the feelings of others, and was able to do so without being shot down. Then a team that could drive change began (slowly) to form.

The details of "Blues versus Greens" may be idiosyncratic, but the basic problem is not at all unusual. Large-scale change does not happen well without a powerful guiding force. A fragmented management team cannot do the job, even if the individual members are strong people. A hero CEO doesn't work either—there aren't enough hours in the day for even the strongest executive to accomplish change single-handedly. Lower-level task forces can be a joke—unless you're on the task force, in which case the joke can be much more painful than funny.

Something else is needed.

The Blues versus the Greens

Seeing

A credible source visibly confronts the issue—there is no "team" guiding the massive integration of two cultures from a merger. He points out, correctly, that there are two competing teams and that the management won't even admit this problem exists, much less try to deal with it. When he does not get shot down for speaking honestly, a few more people also start to talk in public about the real issues.

Feeling

People are shocked. Then some, for the first time, begin to feel optimistic that they can finally deal with the problem. Frustration and anger start to go down.

Changing and Seeing It

Slowly and tentatively the guiding group starts to have honest conversations about the problem. These conversations are far from easy, but they happen, and they happen live, not by memo, so each person in the group gets to see the interaction.

Feeling

Distrust between members of the two groups starts to decrease. Optimism creeps up; anger continues down.

Changing

The group that must guide change begins, for the first time, to act less as two teams and more as one.

Putting Together an Effective Guiding Team

A powerful guiding group has two characteristics. It is made up of the right people, and it demonstrates teamwork. By the "right people," we mean individuals with the appropriate skills, the leadership capacity, the organizational credibility, and the connections to handle a specific kind of organizational change. We do not mean "good individuals" in any generic sense. Nor do we necessarily mean the existing senior management committee.

Many factors contribute to putting the wrong people in charge, with history being the most fundamental. Mergers, as in "Blues/Greens," can leave politically constructed groups at the top. Too much success can leave cronies of cronies running an organization. But instead of confronting the residue of history and making the appropriate changes, we often duck the issues. We leave an inappropriate group in charge, or we dump the work elsewhere. In a pessimistic or cynical mood, we might think that organizational politics inevitably dictate ducking and dumping. But that's not so.

The New and More Diverse Team

From Tom Spector

Until recently, our company was on an acquisition spree, buying large competitors and merging them into our operations. It was a business model that we became very successful with and that produced substantial growth for the company. But now, we've hit the point where there is no one else left to buy. The remaining competitors in the industry are behemoths that are too large to acquire. As a result, our company is grappling with how to transform itself from an organization reliant on growth through acquisition and assimilation to an organization focused on organic growth. This has required us to contemplate changes to both the internal workings of the company and to the way we service the customer.

The team that had been in charge did a great job with the old, acquisition-focused business model. But with the switch, things began to change. I remember sitting in a café last fall with one of our senior people. He said to me in a soft voice, "Before we used to get a deal done and then work like hell to make it work. It was exciting. Now there's none of that." I think the whole team was feeling a bit this way. The intellectual work of deal making and the adrenaline rush were gone. Now it was communicating constantly to large groups of our employees. It was being visible and not secretive. It was dealing with all the many soft issues and with a much greater need to empower others to do the work.

The deal-maker group, and other management committees in the recent past, had been small and like-minded. This was just the way it was done. They were dominated by people with hundreds of years of combined banking experience who often thought and looked alike. So we had a small and homogeneous group of deal makers in a big and heterogeneous company making a huge transition to internal growth.

If Jack, our COO, had let the flow flow, we probably would have still ended up with a small group of people with similar experiences and skills, even if he had switched a few individuals to move from external growth to internal. I'm sure there were some people, maybe many people, who expected this is the way it would be, and should be. That's not what happened.

I still remember receiving the call from his secretary to inform me that Jack wanted to meet. "I'd like you to participate in our operating committee," he told me. "You have a unique perspective that I think is going to help us mold the future of the company." I was surprised and honored. The management committee? I was very excited to become part of this team. He added, "You have an opportunity on this team to create our future. We probably only have a short time to do this before the industry moves beyond this period of transition.

It's a once-in-a-career opportunity that you should embrace." It was a very inspiring meeting and I signed up on the spot. I was committed to making this work before we even had the first operating committee session.

If I didn't fully appreciate why I was being asked to join this group, it began to sink in when we first got together. There was incredible, and calculated, diversity in the room. I mean astonishing. Every major function in the company was represented—finance, human resources, corporate affairs, and IT. He also chose four regional leaders and one from asset management. He chose one of the four key leaders out of the International Commercial Finance Group—a man who had recently worked for Goldman Sachs before joining us. He picked people at different levels, not just people who reported to him. Overall, the group was full of different perspectives and backgrounds. It was diverse not only in skills but also in the mix. We represented the entire company.

It's been a challenging group to manage. But with leadership from Jack and others, so far we're doing it. With that much diversity you can't expect everyone to easily agree, but that's the point. In a typical exchange, I'll say something like, "The only way we can grow is to spend money on career development. We need to invest in developing an online learning program. Our people need new and different skills to be successful in our transforming organization." This, of course, runs counter to what John, one of our corporate finance guys, believes. "I disagree. We need to drive down our costs and trim head count. We can worry about development later. First we need to streamline." Of course, to some extent we're both right. So we have to think and talk. Ultimately, we usually get to a more balanced and creative solution.

We're still early in our transformation, but so far this group seems to be working extremely well, doing what we had more or less hoped. We're beginning to move in a direction that makes much more sense for the new conditions in which we live. The group driving this is bringing a fresh perspective to shaping the future. It is bringing a perspective that is less biased or parochial than you normally see, more creative in shaping what needs to come next. And, with its firm-wide credibility, it has a capacity to communicate powerfully to all parts of the organization. This will become very important some-time soon when we have a lot of important news to communicate.

People let the flow flow all the time. The net result is often a group without the right characteristics, which means a group without the power to make the transformation happen, even if the individuals involved are "good" people.

In most highly successful change efforts, as in this story, effective guiding groups are created in the following way:

1. A single individual who feels great urgency usually pulls in the first people.

2. Individuals are selected to have the right combination of capabilities within the team:

    • Relevant knowledge about what is happening outside the enterprise or group (essential for creating vision)

    • Credibility, connections, and stature within the organization (essential in communicating vision)

    • Valid information about the internal workings of the enterprise (essential for removing the barriers that disempower people from acting on the vision)

    • Formal authority and the managerial skills associated with planning, organizing, and control (needed to create the short-term wins)

    • The leadership skills associated with vision, communication, and motivation (required for nearly every aspect of the change process)

3. The team is created by pulling people in and occasionally pushing people out.

   • *Pulling* means just that—showing others the importance of the effort and the privilege of being chosen. People then understand why they have been selected. More important, their hearts are usually touched. So they feel inspired, which leads to an excited acceptance—not "Oh no, another task force!" In highly successful change, this happens even if the membership of the group has been in place for some time. People are still "pulled into" a guiding team for the change effort.

   • In a similar way, when the strains of a new diverse group develop, people are pulled back together with acts that engender a sense of faith and commitment. In "The New and More Diverse Team," Jack was the central person in displaying these acts at first, then he received help from others.

   • If the makeup of the group is wrong, *pushing* means taking steps to correct the problem, even if that means firing someone or performing other difficult, emotion-packed actions. The status quo and momentum from the past do not win.

4. As change progresses throughout large organizations, additional groups are formed at lower levels. These teams help drive action within their units. With multiple levels of drivers, the term *guiding coalition* may be more appropriate than *guiding team* because groups of 50 or 500 are rarely teams in any sense that we normally use the word. If a leap into the future is for only one unit in a big organization, or for all of a small enterprise, then one guiding team may be sufficient.

All too often, this pattern is not found—not even close. The task force problem is pervasive. You see this often with systems projects. A firm's executive committee approves the expenditure of tens of millions of dollars and then hands the responsibility and accountability over to a twelve-person task force staffed mostly by people buried in the organization. Ask the execs about this approach and they say, "Those are the people who understand the technology. So they must be in charge." The members of the task force try to do the job. But they are not expected to create a vision, and they don't. When they do try to communicate something about their objectives or plan, it is ignored or not seen as credible by many people. When they start to bump into barriers—a threatened middle management, the wrong compensation formulas, a resisting executive vice president—they become frustrated and look to someone above them to solve these problems. Top management is preoccupied elsewhere—this is not their job, they are not the software people—so they do little and do it slowly. Others do less, since no one wants to make sacrifices for this task force, especially with the hanging question "If this change is so important, why aren't the real bosses guiding the effort?"

Realizing the problems with individuals and weak committees, frustrated systems consultants are often pushed into creating complex governance structures full of sponsors, cross-functional task forces, ownership teams or owners, and the like. These complex structures are usually an improvement over a single weak committee, which is why people use them. But this approach usually works poorly. Complicated governance systems are never at the core of the enterprise, where the real power lies. They are overlays on top of the existing formal and informal relationships that make the organization function. Using this approach is like sitting on the roof of a house and trying to stick an incredibly complex mechanism down the chimney to move the furniture around. Also, all too often these overlays are staffed by people who already have full-time jobs. When these people discover that the structure will not work well and that they will receive little credit for their extra effort, they often invest a minimum of time and energy. Without that investment, the structure works even less well. And complex overlays usually add much too much bureaucracy. That slows down decision making. At the extreme, this begins to look silly. It's rather like a family whose problem is that the children need new skills, and whose proposed solution is a project team at the state's Child Services Agency working in conjunction with the Department of Education and the Governor's Task Force on New Skills.

Even when the "what" is understood, the "how" can become mechanistic in ways that fail. "You are on the new team. Here is the agenda. Your job is X and Y." Not addressed are queries full of affect: "But what's the purpose? Can we succeed? What will this demand of me? Can I supply what will be demanded? What about the implications to my career if we do not succeed?" In "New Team," Jack seems to have been sensitive to these issues. He addressed the feelings—softening the negatives (suspicion, fear) and inspiring the positives (optimism, pride). In "Blues/Greens," a retreat to an overly intellectualized discussion about "values" missed the point.

Unlike many challenges in life, these problems can often be avoided with insight. It's not a tornado, which is out of your control. People *create* guiding team problems. Once you see the issues, you can steer clear of the pitfalls. That's the power of insight. The division president can learn and use the lessons. The employee two levels down can help the division president learn the lessons. But if you are two levels down, remember, finding a way to *show* the boss the issues is much more powerful than a valid but boring memo.

The Issue of Trust

The right group of people is necessary but insufficient. The group must also work together well. Here the key issue seems to be one of trust.

Trust is often missing in senior management teams, although top managers are loath to admit this in public. If the individuals do not need to work together closely, because the work is routine or because the changes are small and can be made slowly, weak trust is not necessarily a problem. With big changes in a fast-moving world, it's a huge problem. How can you create a sensible vision and strategies for the overall group in a team with low trust? People will think of themselves or of their subgroups first and be protective and suspicious. Smart strategy does not emerge from a pond full of politics, parochialism, and guarded communication.

Here's an extreme case of the problem, and a solution. After reading the first two paragraphs, what would you have predicted was possible?

General Mollo and I Were Floating in the Water

From Roland de Vries

The war was over and we knew we had to work together somehow. It was a negotiated peace, not a military victory where one side could impose its will on the other. There was a new nation, and a new army, to build. I was charged with leading a team of officers to develop a vision, strategy, and implementation plan for the merger of the seven armies into one National Defense Force.

We brought together the representatives from the seven groups that made up the new South African Army. The seven were the Defense Force of the apartheid regime, two liberation armies, and four armies from the homelands. They had been on opposite sides of a long and bitter struggle from which I still carry a few physical scars from a land mine that virtually destroyed the command vehicle I was in. We had been enemies and now we were suddenly being asked to work together to create a unified organization.

The initial meeting was difficult, but not in the way you might think. We were professional soldiers. There was no shouting or shoving. In some ways, it was just the opposite, which maybe was worse. We *sounded* cooperative. "Our new situation requires a new order with a new vision. In order to develop a new vision we need to become trusting, truthful, and candid." The words were nice, but they were clearly just words.

Everyone was cautious, feeling each other out. There was no trust, no truth, and no candor. I doubt if anyone said what was on his mind. Why would you expect anything else? But with the history and the suspicions, I could imagine this group meeting for a year and nothing much changing. More likely, everything would get worse. When the meetings did not resolve anything, or resolve it fast enough, people would start to blame others. That's only human. They would huddle more and more with their groups. It was clear that all the terrible hate and pain could resurface, and then what would happen?

At our second meeting I made a very personal decision. I felt I had to do what I thought was right in this situation. I could not see how we could create one organization unless we could somehow learn to be trustful and candid with each other. Of course it would be difficult. But what was the alternative? So I told them some truth about my situation: "Key people on our side want the new army to be just like our old National Defense Force. They do not want to merge all the elements. They expect me to make everyone else to be like them." I ended my comments by saying "I have no intention of doing that. It does not make sense to me. It is wrong, and I will not do it."

You could say that this was insane. Many things could have happened—less in the meeting than over the following week—that would not have been helpful to the group or to me personally. But was that not the right thing to do? If you spend all your life calculating what is safest, is it a good life?

The conversation could have turned in a number of different directions immediately after my comments. What actually happened was this: Others began to tell similar stories! It did not happen fast, but one person also took a risk, then another. Someone admitted, "I too have people who want no real merging." Another said, "I have people who want everything to be on their terms. They want the new vision to be their old vision." And so on. Not everyone spoke up, but it was still amazing.

With that meeting, we made our first small step in the right direction.

One of the things we then did to get to know each other on a personal basis was to have regular camping trips, which everyone on the team came to enjoy. At night we would sit around an open fire telling war stories. Some of my new colleagues were able to do this more comfortably than others, but we did it. After a few of these, we actually discussed the various battle strategies we used when we were fighting each other. We would also break into smaller groups and just go off and talk to get to know each other on a deeper level.

The "moment of truth" incident for us happened when a boat capsized in the sea, throwing me and Solly Mollo overboard. Solly was a senior commander with the Spear of the Nation liberation army. The two of us were floating in our life jackets for a while when he looked at me and said, "I can't swim." I looked at him and said, "You should not worry because I am a strong swimmer, and I can and will take care of you until we reach the shore." Can you imagine how this must have looked, the two of us hanging onto each other in the open sea?

We floated for over an hour before we were rescued. In order to pass the time, we shared stories with each other. I don't remember how we got started, but our tales were very personal. We talked about our families and the sacrifices they had to make as a result of our being soldiers. We talked about our feelings on the racial problems that had been pulling our country apart. We talked about issues we faced in bringing two very different cultures together.

The candid conversations, talk around the campfires, floating in the water—many things, by both design and chance, pulled us together. And it is rather amazing, in my opinion, what can happen to a group of enemies.

When we throw up our hands and declare that in *our* situation the teamwork problems are hopelessly difficult, it is useful to remember this story.

Here is a dramatic example of the basic method by which trust is established, no matter the situation. Its lessons include:

- Show people what is needed through modeling (in this story, for example, taking a risk in the second meeting).

- Act in a way that is fiery, that hits the emotions (e.g., "It is wrong and I will not do it").

- As behavior starts to change, add new activities in a different setting (e.g., sitting around the campfire).

- When a "moment of truth" event happens, grab it, then turn it into a story that is told vividly and dramatically, so that it will be passed along to as many people as possible (e.g., clinging to each other while floating in the sea).

- Through all of these steps, help people believe and feel that change is possible, that they can work together, and that a great organization can be built.

People do this in settings far less dramatic than "General Mollo." The protagonists of "Blues/Greens" followed the same basic pattern: The first two points can be seen in the meeting at the university, and the last three in the follow-up to that session.

The key is not "organization" in a managerial sense. Although we often say "Those people need to get organized," here it isn't a matter of formal authority or obedience to status. Both are weak ties if trust is absent. And weakness is a killer when guiding teams go through a big change.

The Mechanics of Meetings

Teamwork, and the underlying feelings of trust and emotional commitment to others, can be undercut by many factors. Individuals who aren't team players or who aren't trustworthy can destroy a group. More subtle, but just as important, is the very mechanical question of meeting format.

How often do you meet and for how long? What is the typical agenda? Who runs the sessions? What work is done outside the formal meetings? Are non–group members welcome? If yes, who and when? Get the format wrong and frustration grows, trust collapses, and you have a guiding team in name only. Get it right and the group pulls together into a sufficiently powerful force to do the work.

Poor meeting structure hurts particularly when a group is new. Smart people make mistakes here all the time. They pull good individuals together, and, because there is some trust and goodwill, they talk about the real issues. They discuss this point, then that one. Then another, and another. Then they go back to the first because it is still important. And they talk and talk— until it starts to drive people nuts.

Meetings Down Under

From Ross Divett

We selected fifty-five people in numerous locations to lead the change in their areas. Our first meeting of this group was held in one of the nicest hotels in downtown Sydney. People from some of our more remote offices arrived on Thursday evening and had the chance to get to know one another and exchange ideas over drinks at the hotel bar. Then on Friday, everyone met in one of the hotel conference rooms for more formal discussion about their roles in leading this change. Our second meeting followed a similar format, but it was held in Melbourne.

There was excitement during the first meetings, and people liked the fact that they had been selected as one of the change effort's key leaders. We discussed the direction of the organization and brainstormed ideas that would help us become more customer focused. But in the second meeting and throughout the third, the discussion started lurching. We'd go one way. Then we'd go another. One person would say, "I have a great idea on how to give our offices a more customer-friendly feel: Let's have our service reps wear name tags, so that customers can get to know them on a first-name basis." Someone else might say, "Yes, and let's redesign our offices so that they're less formal. Let's have seating areas for our customers to read about our services, and give each service rep their own desk." Then somebody else would pipe in with, "I don't think that having our service reps wear name tags, or redesigning our offices, will really change the way we work. The first thing we need to do is scrap our 900-page HR policy manuals." That comment would be counterargued with, "No, no. To really get our employees to change their focus, we need to put in new performance measures. We need to start rewarding people differently."

Everyone had their own ideas about where we should be focusing, so we'd get onto this issue, then off to that one. With all of this jumping around, we couldn't get into any substantive detail, which was frustrating. We tried to have group votes to determine our top priorities, but that didn't get us anywhere either. Initial enthusiasm for the work drained fast. In a way, the group was still locked into its old command-and-control style. And we were all trying to command and control one another!

On about our fifth session, we tried a new approach. To begin, we scheduled our meeting for a day and a half, as opposed to just one day. When the team arrived, we gave them a detailed schedule of the next two days' activities. At the top of the schedule, one issue was listed: performance management.

The CEO began the first day's activities by stressing how important it was that the group change its focus and work together to reach consensus. She said that we were going to try something new. She said that we had discussed many good ideas, but that it was now time to get to work. From here on out, we would discuss one major issue per meeting, which would last a day and a half. When necessary, we would use a facilitator to help us stay on track.

The rest of the morning began with a guest speaker who talked about the various ways to approach performance management. That started us thinking outside of our own little worlds and gave us new ideas. We then flagged critical issues for changing our performance management system. We used the afternoon to discuss what needed to be done next. We decided that we would begin by surveying employees to determine areas they'd like to see improved.

On day two, we addressed the timeline we were operating under and broke up some of the work that needed to be done over the next couple of weeks. We also identified what most people thought the next meeting's key issue should be, then agreed to have certain team members create discussion documents that would be distributed one week before the next meeting.

We continued to use this format for the rest of our sessions. They were always a day and a half long. Day one always involved a guest speaker; day two always addressed concrete next steps. Complex issues were assigned to subgroups for more analysis and planning. These subgroups would then report their progress back to the entire group during the next meeting.

It took a couple of sessions for the group to get used to this format, but we soon discovered that whenever we drifted from this formula, we were not as effective.

If an outsider were to attend our meetings now they'd likely be surprised at how little we get sidetracked, at the level of attendance even though people are busy and have to travel, and at how few disruptive sidebar conversations there are. And over time this format has become easier as people have learned to trust the process, and each other.

It took us nine months to turn this big and geographically dispersed group into an effective team, but the payoff has been substantial. We're creating an entirely new organization.

Bad meetings undermine trust, especially with a new group. Here we see a simple, well-known, yet clever approach to this problem. The key is focus and discipline. Have one topic per meeting. Do your homework to better launch the work. Make sure the next steps are clear. Put someone credible in charge. In "Down Under," this formula resulted in better discussions, which reduced frustration. Less frustration helped build the trust that supports teamwork.

This simple but effective formula was not started with a discussion and vote on the format. It was started, mostly, with a demonstration of its power. People could see it work.

The same rules apply in smaller and older groups. Every situation will have its peculiarities that may demand additional or slightly different methods. But the key point is simple: Make sure the formula has been thought out clearly and is not only a product of history.

Overlap among the Eight Steps

In "Down Under" we see an example of how the eight steps overlap, how the sequence is not start step 1, finish step 1, start step 2, finish step 2, and so on. While the Australians were still developing the sort of guiding team that could transform their organization, they began the work of developing a change vision and strategies. They didn't just have a year of "team building" meetings.

A similar overlap can often be found across steps 1 and 2. You are still building urgency among people in general while you begin creating the guiding team in a group that now has a relatively low complacency level. With steps 4 and 5, you are still communicating the change vision to people in general while you start to empower action on that vision among people who now have bought in. With steps 5 and 6, you are still destroying obstacles to action while you are organizing for short-term wins within channels where the obstacles are gone.

You always have to be cautious that you don't recklessly jump ahead. Trying to empower people who don't feel much urgency doesn't work. Trying to produce a third wave of change with no short-term wins won't work. Nevertheless, some overlap in stages is normal.

When the Bosses Seem Hopeless

Just as the CEO in "Down Under" took control of the meetings, so too the boss in charge of any unit to be changed—a division or a department—has to be a central force in the guiding team. For the sake of the credibility of the effort, and to avoid the constant threat of the boss pulling the plug on the change, this is essential. Trying to dance around the most powerful figure is futile. Nevertheless, determined people do try. They try to prop up the boss, sort of giving him or her cue cards. They try to run around the boss, create their own guiding team with like-minded friends, and then rush ahead to create a vision. But none of this ever works well.

Those who know these facts often retreat. "George can't do it," they say. "So what can I do? Be realistic."

When we run around or retreat, we miss an essential point. If key players are not playing key roles in the guiding team, that usually means their sense of urgency is too low and their complacency or anger or fear too high. Perhaps the organization has been very successful—hence, complacency. Perhaps the boss seriously wonders if he or she can lead a big change and survive— hence, fear. Under those circumstances, the change effort needs to focus on this issue and this issue *alone*. Forget the team and teamwork (step 2). Forget vision (step 3). Forget communication (step 4) and empowerment (step 5). The only issue is urgency (step 1). Period. When the problem is framed this way, we can see how almost anyone can be of help. Remember "Gloves."

Yes, the executive vice president can help, but so can the first-line supervisor. So can the staff professional with no subordinates. So can the consultants. So can a summer student! The key is focusing on the right issue.

This is a very important point, and one we miss all the time. Watch out!

Build the Guiding Team

Help form a group that has the capability—in membership and method of operating—to guide a very difficult change process.

WHAT WORKS

- Showing enthusiasm and commitment (or helping someone do so) to help draw the right people into the group
- Modeling the trust and teamwork needed in the group (or helping someone to do that)
- Structuring meeting formats for the guiding team so as to minimize frustration and increase trust
- Putting your energy into step 1 (raising urgency) if you cannot take on the step 2 challenge and if the right people will not

WHAT DOES NOT WORK

- Guiding change with weak task forces, single individuals, complex governance structures, or fragmented top teams
- Not confronting the situation when momentum and entrenched power centers undermine the creation of the right group
- Trying to leave out or work around the head of the unit to be changed because he or she is "hopeless"

STORIES TO REMEMBER

- The Blues versus the Greens
- The New and More Diverse Team
- General Mollo and I Were Floating in the Water
- Meetings Down Under

STEP ONE
Increase Urgency

STEP TWO
Build the Guiding Team

STEP THREE
Get the Vision Right

STEP FOUR
Communicate for Buy-In

STEP FIVE
Empower Action

STEP SIX
Create Short-Term Wins

STEP SEVEN
Don't Let Up

STEP EIGHT
Make Change Stick

STEP 3

Get the
Vision Right

I N SUCCESSFUL LARGE-SCALE CHANGE, a well-functioning guiding team answers the questions required to produce a clear sense of direction. What change is needed? What is our vision of the new organization? What should not be altered? What is the best way to make the vision a reality? What change strategies are unacceptably dangerous? Good answers to these questions position an organization to leap into a better future.

Far too often, guiding teams either set no clear direction or embrace visions that are not sensible. The consequences can be catastrophic for organizations and painful for employees—just ask anyone who has suffered through a useless fad forced on them from above.

Visions and Strategies versus Plans and Budgets

One reason that smart people create no or poor direction for change is because they have been taught that "charting the future" means planning and budgeting. Truth is, when pursuing large-scale change, the best planning exercise is never sufficient. Something very different is essential.

Painting Pictures of the Future

From Charles Berry

In 1994, we knew we were on the brink of having to redefine what we wanted to be as a business. Major structural changes were starting to happen within our industry due to deregulation—opening up our marketplace to competitors and ending our protection from being acquired by other firms. Deregulation and liberalization of the UK market meant, firstly, overseas competition was coming in and, secondly, there was a chance for us to start expanding overseas through acquisition.

Everyone had their own opinion of what we needed to do, and they didn't all agree. Some people felt we should become a diversified conglomerate, maybe like a Hanson, the largest UK conglomerate. Others felt we should be an engineering company, where we would effectively become contractors, building and maintaining water, gas, and electricity networks. Still others believed we needed to move further into telecommunications and Internet services.

Our CEO at the time had tried to wrestle with this. He had sent a memo to the heads of our major divisions asking them for their views and asking them to suggest our options for the future. It was a very orthodox planning process. The division heads responded. All their ideas and suggestions were pulled together by somebody in our head office and they, of course, ran all the numbers for each of the suggestions. What landed back on the desk of the division heads was a very dry report with a ton of financial information—yards and yards of spreadsheet analysis on debt/equity ratios, share price, performance indices—the sort of stuff that sends most people to sleep very quickly! A year later people were still discussing the report, generally starting the conversation with "What was figure 3.4 all about?" This would be followed by an exciting discussion of figure 3.4. No real agreement could be reached. People just didn't have a good sense of what the options were and what they would mean for us.

An "orthodox planning exercise," as you find it in most organizations, is designed for incremental change. Typically, everyone involved knows their business in some detail. It doesn't take much to imagine options that are a little different one way or the other. Planning and budgeting forces you to think through the details. It allows you to say "Given what we know, a 5.3 percent revenue growth target is sensible. To achieve that goal, asking Fred to head the X project over the next quarter is a good idea. The Y project will logically be required, and its short-term costs in the coming fiscal year are affordable in light of competing demands for cash."

With large-scale change, extrapolating from the current, known context is not easy. People typically do not comprehend all the relevant options, or at least not very clearly. What does it mean to "change all the business processes?" What does it mean to become a "global" corporation? What does it mean to create "a more innovative culture"? You can't plan for what you don't understand. You often have difficulty even having a good discussion of the issues. "We need to have a culture that promotes risk taking." "Well, yes, I suppose, but risk taking means some errors, and our customers defect to competitors when we make mistakes." "I didn't mean risky risk." "Risky risk?!"

Often we retreat into the seeming objectivity of numbers. But with nonincremental change, financial analysis has to begin with specific alternatives and then has to be based on assumptions that are often hard to make or, again, hard to talk about.

To help us grapple with this problem of how to redefine our business, we began by picking six or seven basic options, six or seven broad visions of the future. One was to carry on as we were—business as usual—supplying electricity to our Scottish customers along with some limited telecommunication and Internet services. A second was to be an electricity provider for the whole UK marketplace, not just Scotland. So we would forget the limited growth opportunities we had identified in the other two areas of business we were currently in. We'd refocus and just do one thing really well. A third was to batten down the hatches completely, retrench, and only provide electricity within Scotland with a view to being acquired by another organization. These three were probably considered, by many of us at the time, as the safer options that we could take. The others were much more expansive: to be an international electricity company; a multi-utility, offering electricity, gas, and water within the UK; a conglomerate; or an engineering company. As we started to discuss these options, another one emerged—to be in Internet services and telecommunications.

When we came to look at this again, we decided to develop some very simple dimensions by which to describe the options:

- SALES TURNOVER—what might be our revenue in ten years' time

- EMPLOYEES—how many employees we would have

- CUSTOMERS—how many customers we would have

- BUSINESSES—what core products or services we would offer

- COMPETITORS—who our major competitors would be

- BELIEFS—what we would have to believe about ourselves to be successful

- ACTION STEPS—what the key actions necessary to achieve this option would be

We put together two or three pages on each possible future. We had financial numbers in there, but for the most part we kept the detailed financial analysis separate. As we went through the options, we tried to paint six pictures of the future and then bring them alive. That was the idea—painting pictures of the future.

We scheduled a series of meetings for the eight-person executive team. Before the first meeting, we sent team members the summary pages so they would have a chance to read the material. When we met, I recapped the main points very quickly, using an overhead projector. So for option 1, international electricity provider, our sales turnover in ten years would be . . . , and on through each of the very simple dimensions we wanted to use. Then we would debate each option. We would ask ourselves, "What would we look like?" "What would be our number one product or service?" "Where might we be located?" "What kind of people would we have?" "What would our ads look like?" "What demands would customers make on us?" "What would we do to respond to those demands?" "What might the plants and offices look like?" "What would we have to do especially well?" "How do we feel about this?"

By trying to visualize the future, it gave us a feeling that went far beyond numbers and abstract opinions. It helped us understand the magnitude of the changes we would have to undertake if we embraced any given option.

Our formal discussions were in four-hour meetings. We narrowed down the options rather quickly. Conglomerate was out, and setting ourselves up to be acquired was out. Where we had identified "multi-utility in the UK" as one option, we began to explore "multi-utility in the world" as another. The pictures we had started were, in some cases, quite extreme, so I think it was natural that people played around with them and created new alternatives. After each meeting my team would put together a summary of the options that were left and what we had concluded about them. The summary was on one page. We sent it to each of the directors. You could almost hear the sigh of relief that they weren't being sent another Excel file or an e-mail with sixteen new attachments. From that point on, we deliberately captured all the feedback after the sessions and summarized it on one page only.

Some common ground began to emerge. "So, we are starting to like the look of an international multi-utility. What would we have to believe about ourselves to know that we would be successful? How would we compete in each of these geographies?" And the process started again. This time, we tested our conclusions each step of the way. We began to focus on the actions that we would take to achieve that vision and whether the financials made sense. We also sent the one-page summaries to our external financial brokers, who gave us some feedback on how they thought the market would respond if we went down each of those roads. We discussed their comments. We started to get more illustrative about the shape of the company, how we would grow, where we would get our financing from. Our finance director said, "We will need to triple the size of our company within five years if we are going to provide our shareholders with a better return than if we had just sold out." Somebody else said, "We could triple in size if we bought an electricity and water company in the UK and then we made one other similar purchase internationally." And then somebody else said, "The pennies just dropped for me! I can now see how we would do this."

Having the financials underneath was necessary. But the pictures were most important in helping us reach a consensus on the vision. They were pictures of possible futures.

Painting Pictures of the Future

Seeing

Someone on the planning staff finds a new approach to planning. With sufficient urgency in the group, a frustrated senior management is willing to try it. The planner works with this guiding team to identify some alternatives (e.g., international energy company), then fleshes each out on a few pages of paper along a limited number of key dimensions. He uses that material to create a discussion that helps others "see" alternative futures.

Feeling

Frustration ("We aren't getting anywhere"), anger ("I can see the direction we need to go; why can't we just do it?"), anxiety ("Will we remake the company into something where my skills won't be relevant?"), and pessimism ("We're going to be acquired whether we like it or not") go down. A sense of relief grows ("Oh, I see what he's talking about. I can see some good alternatives now"). Optimism grows ("It could be a very interesting company").

Changing

They start to have much more productive conversations. They start to make decisions about an intelligent vision of the future.

In cases of successful large-scale change, you find four elements that help direct action: budgets, plans, strategies, and visions. All four are different yet tightly interrelated, and each requires a different development process.

A *budget* is the financial piece of the plan. A *plan* specifies step by step how to implement a strategy. A *strategy* shows how to achieve a vision. A *vision* shows an end state where all the plans and strategies will eventually take you. A vision can usually fit on a page and be described in an elevator ride. A strategy might take ten pages and require a discussion over a meal. Plans could fit into a notebook and require examination in a series of meetings. Budgets could require a large notebook and demand even more meetings.

A guiding team never creates all four elements by itself. Others help. As in "Painting Pictures," sometimes those others are critical not just in providing information used in the process, but also in helping create the right process.

Budgeting is a math exercise, number crunching. Planning is a logical, linear process. Strategizing requires a great deal of information about customers and competitors, along with conceptual skills. Visioning uses a very different part of the brain than budgeting. As the name implies, it involves trying to see possible futures. It inevitably has both a creative and emotional component (e.g., "How do we *feel* about the options?"). When you use "orthodox planning" to create a vision, frustration and failure are inevitable.

With incremental change, visions and strategies are often so obvious that you don't even think about them. All the work goes into exercises that create plans and budgets. With large-scale change, visions and strategies are the hard part because they require venturing into unknown territory. And if they're not set correctly, you're dead.

Without a good budget, you can run out of money. Without a sensible plan, you can run out of time. Without a good strategy, you can find yourself painted into a corner. Without a good vision, you can choose a bad direction and never realize that you've done so. You will have difficulty coordinating large numbers of people without using endless directives. You'll never get the energy needed to accomplish something very difficult. Strategic plans motivate few people, but a compelling vision can appeal to the heart and motivate anyone.

The efficient coordinating function of vision is directly related to the issue of speed. In a slow-moving world, a team can walk slowly with blindfolds, guided by standards, without tripping over each other. The team moves in unison, with their feet going left-right-left at a well known cadence. If the lead person runs into a wall, she says "Stop" (probably after "Ouch"). Then she considers the situation and makes a new plan. The plan is communicated— "We all turn 90 degrees to the left, take two steps, then stop. I (the boss) will use my right hand to see if the barrier is still on my right. Then we. . . ." Now imagine a world in which the winners have to run and dodge walls, and do so quickly. Without vision, and without everyone having the same vision, running into obstacles and tripping over one another is inevitable.

The problem of setting direction well, or poorly, during a large-scale change is closely related to history. Accounting has been taught to managers in modern organizations for many decades. Planning became more of a systematic tool in the middle of the twentieth century. Strategy was not a word used in business school curricula until the late 1970s. Vision is still not a serious subject in most of managerial training. Is it surprising what we tend to do well and what we tend to do poorly?

Efficiency versus Service

No vision issue today is bigger than the question of efficiency versus some combination of innovation and customer service.

With the pressures on enterprises everywhere, costs have become a huge problem. Many transformations have at their heart a belt-tightening vision. If you're bleeding to death, a short-term cost turnaround has to be the focus. But in many situations, enterprises are not bleeding to death, yet the vision is squarely centered on achieving much lower expenses. When this view of the future is sensible—it sometimes is not—it can still work poorly as a vision because most people have great difficulty becoming excited about slashing expenses. Fear, anger, and cynicism grow. Change is slowed, resisted.

There is a way around this problem, and it's not ignoring costs. It's crafting service-oriented visions that are impossible to achieve without actions that significantly reduce unnecessary expenses.

Cost versus Service

From Ron Bingham

A vision focused on cutting costs, streamlining the organization, or efficiency just wouldn't fly. For the most part, our people saw themselves as being here for the entire community, for the public, for what they saw as the greater common good. That's the way they talked. "We're not here to make a profit but to provide essential services to the public." For the most part, they really believed this, often deeply. And they were certainly not here to make a lot of money for themselves. That is not the nature of state government, and we all knew that.

But here's the rub: The governor saw a lot of waste that had built up over the years. He felt strongly that the public could not, should not, be funding inefficiencies. For him, the bottom line was saving money so the government could increase funding in key areas like education. For my piece of the action, he assumed the vision would have to be one of saving money. When I began, I was of a similar mind.

So we have two trains on the same track coming at each other. Efficiency is the issue; efficiency is not our mission. After a lot of thought and discussion, I finally figured out that we could and should have a vision of customer service. The idea was not to abandon the efficiencies issue, but to think about it differently, focus it differently. The staff thinks in terms of providing essential services. Most would really like to provide better service. They aren't fools. They can see that the public is not running around saying "Wow, is the state government great. I mean, move over Federal Express and Wal-Mart, these guys have got it." Since increased funding was a total impossibility, you couldn't achieve better service with more money. So what is the only option? Removing impediments to better service. And removing impediments in the bureaucracy inevitably leads to taking out wasted money. It follows logically.

So we chose the services vision. When we communicated that, and did so as clearly as possible, people could almost see themselves helping others the way they wanted to help others. They could almost see a citizen of this state thanking them for their good work. I think most employees honestly became inspired with the opportunity to truly improve the way they could serve the public. Stand aside, cynics—it really happened. The response was incredible. We suddenly had people throughout the organization examining what they did and thinking about how they could offer better service. I remember we had a meeting in front of the governor and his senior team where employees were presenting their visions of how their departments would operate in the future. The social services presentation was especially inspirational. This woman stands up and says, "Our vision is a future where we will deal with you as a whole person, as a whole family. We'll take care of your food stamps, your training. We'll help you so you can have a healthy vital family. You will feel cared for and treated with respect." The passion with which she spoke was unbelievable. She was committed and believed in that vision. She was going to make sure these people were helped. And of course to do that meant ripping apart the organization. Tearing down all the duplicative practices that had people filling out the same forms ten times whenever they interacted with social services. All that would have to go, and so would some jobs along with it. But that didn't matter as much as community service, as much as helping people who can't help themselves.

A group from the revenue department presented a future state where people could call in with a question about a tax return and not have to wait on the phone for an hour. Even better, people could get the information they required fast with no follow-up. This from the revenue service! Can you imagine? To do this meant the purchase of new technology—which, of course, can be expensive and would have to be offset by job changes, either transfers out of the organization or into other departments. But the new system, if done right, could be much more efficient, and, over time, save a lot of money.

All this created some disruptions. Because people were committed to improving service, most were willing to put up with that. Of course, not everyone felt this way, but enough did.

The result was, a few years into this, that we saved more money than the governor ever dreamed possible. It blew him away. It blew *me* away. And, we got more of what was also needed—better service. The right vision made all the difference in the world.

In many places today you have the same problem. Costs are bloated but the workforce cannot relate to an "efficiency" vision. In some cases, the complications are greater than in this story. The workforce may be convinced that more money is available. The management may be unwilling to invest in information technology. The bosses may think customer service is just fine. But in many cases, the vision and supporting strategies are simply wrong. The vision is too narrow—it doesn't see the whole enterprise or consider all the relevant relationships. Instead it feels like a mean budget. So anger and fear grow. A vision that creates anger and fear among a significant number of people will never work.

The solution in "Cost versus Service" can be used in many places. The cynics are wrong: Most of us get a great feeling from helping other people. So you make the vision service-oriented, something with which people can identify. You put blasting the bad system at the core of the strategy. When people embrace these ends and means, costs disappear as a consequence *and* you get better service. This idea can work in manufacturing businesses, high-tech firms, financial services—nearly anywhere.

Bold Strategies for Bold Visions

In an accelerating world, change visions are becoming bolder by necessity. More and more executives now believe that their visions must include being an industry leader, being a firm that is first into new markets, or being the low-cost competitor. Bold visions require bold strategies, and here is where the process breaks down. Fine, let's be the best, or the first, or the lowest-cost producer. But how? People without a great deal of bold strategy development experience often flounder. They can't figure out what to do because it's different from anything they have done before. They sometimes back away from the obvious because it's threatening. Or they convince themselves that small modifications in their current ways of operating will achieve the vision—eventually. Or, because they can think of no strategic possibility, they conclude that the vision is ridiculous, even though it is not.

The Plane Will Not Move!

From Debbie Collard

A C-17 is a huge aircraft. Its tail rises four stories. Watching it being built is an incredible thing.

Aircraft are typically assembled in a series of locations within one manufacturing facility, locations we call "positions." You start work in one place, then when a set of tasks are completed, you move the plane to a second, and then another until you're done. In the case of the C-17, the main fuselage might be assembled in position A, the tail attached over in position B, the wings attached in position C, the cockpit electronics installed in position D, and so on. For this, you have to have a hangar that's large enough for two or three 747-sized aircraft to be in production, along with the equipment. This is a huge amount of square footage. Fifteen hundred of our employees would be in this giant hangar. They would be dealing with many, many thousands of parts. It's an incredible production process that requires complex scheduling and coordination.

The speed with which an airplane moves through the different positions is driven by the schedule. If work is not complete at one position when the schedule says it should move, or if needed parts don't arrive in time, the plane moves anyway and the unfinished work is done at the end. As you can imagine, taking apart a plane at the end of the line, adding parts, and then reassembling leads to quality problems and delays. But this was the way the whole industry did things. No one questioned it. I suppose it was like third-grade children going to school from 8:00 to 3:00 and sitting in rooms with teachers. Of course you do it that way.

As soon as Koz arrived, he made it clear that the priorities for the C-17 program were to excel in terms of quality, schedule, and cost, in that order. He really raised the bar, setting a clear vision of the significantly improved performance we needed. I bet he talked to everyone about this and got much head-nodding. "Sure, boss." And I bet most people wanted that vision and did try a little harder. But many accepted the existing basic production system as the only way to do things, and with that they accepted certain problems as inevitable. The mind-set was, "Yeah, it would be nice if we were never out of needed parts but that's impossible in this industry." So while people made small adjustments, the overall production strategy did not come close to achieving Koz's raised-bar vision.

Then one day he stood up in a management meeting and made

an announcement. "We are not going to move an airplane until it is complete in position. Quality is number one, so that's what we are going to focus on. Until the plane is done and done right, no movement. Period."

Everyone thought he was off his rocker. You didn't do things this way. I think some of his direct reports, in particular, thought he was crazy. They were convinced that we would never be able to deliver on time if we did it this way. Never. Wouldn't happen, anybody knows that. Something would always bring everything to a halt. You'd have employees twiddling their thumbs at great expense to the company. You might as well expect cars to be made by secretaries on the fifty-ninth floor of the Sears building in Chicago.

We had all heard the quality speech before, but here was a guy telling us that nothing goes anywhere unless it's properly done. Koz showed complete conviction that this radical idea was right. And if his words didn't win us over, all day long we had to look at a plane that was not moving until it was complete in a position. All day long, there it was, not moving. Nope. Sitting there.

After Koz made his proclamation, things began to change faster. The fact that out-of-position work would not be tolerated meant that suddenly having parts arrive on time was critical. Our procurement guys got motivated like I'd never seen before. They started coming up with all kinds of new change strategies for their operation. And—incredible since this couldn't be done—they started succeeding in getting our suppliers to operate in new ways. So we began getting the right parts at the right time! Overall, people just didn't want to be the reason that a plane was held in position for longer than it was supposed to. They didn't want to be embarrassed, they didn't want to hurt the company, they didn't want to hurt their careers, and they didn't want to let Koz down. So they started breaking through walls. As evidence began to accumulate that this nutty idea might actually be working, more people got with the program. More started finding ways to punch through walls. When they couldn't do it by themselves, they would come to Koz with specific ideas,

> sometimes very clever ideas, for what was needed and for how problems could be solved. Koz would then work with them to remove the obstacles. So if it helped for Koz to talk to the president of a parts company, he'd do it.
>
> Holding the planes in place eliminated all sorts of bad habits. No longer could we say, "Of course some percentage of parts won't arrive on time. That's just life." No, that's not life. That's life as we knew it.
>
> To make a long story short, we transformed the place, and, as a result, quality has gone up and all of our aircraft have not only been on time, they've been early!
>
> To this day people still tell this story, from the shop floor to the executive offices. "He said the plane would not move. Period."

If Koz hadn't had enough respect and credibility among his direct reports, if they did not feel some sense of urgency or if they thought the new vision was nonsense, this approach would have failed. The foundation would not have been there, and people would have devised many clever ways to undermine the boss. But with the early steps in the change process having been done minimally well, and with his actions probably raising the sense of urgency, a bold strategy helped make the bold vision a reality.

Imagine what might have happened in this sort of situation—and often does. Scenario 1: Koz might have never tried something so bold. He might have continued to talk and talk. His people would have continued to say "Sure, boss." No bold strategies would have been developed. The vision would not have been achieved. Scenario 2: If Koz became louder and applied more pressure, the frustration, anger, and fear would have grown. He might have demanded that people send him new strategic plans. They could easily have gone into a group conspiracy. "Logical" plans would have been submitted full of old ideas. Eventually

Koz would have backed off, either because he was convinced they were right or out of total frustration. Scenario 3: As the frustration and anger grew in the workforce, preventing the development of new strategies, Koz might have become more frustrated and angry, creating a nasty cycle that would, in some way, eventually blow up. Scenario 4: The pessimists and cynics might have quickly won the day, probably by convincing sufficient people that Koz was a good man but naive, or was a bad man seeking only to further his career. Sometimes we think one of these negative scenarios is inevitable. But that's not true.

Notice how it actually worked in this case. The unmoving plane was a huge visual reminder that new action was needed and expected or there would be a disaster with who-knew-what consequences. Change enthusiasts on the staff probably uncorked champagne. "Now we're going somewhere!" Others learned quickly that the same old routine would lead to disaster—for the plant and maybe for them. So, many people started trying to develop new strategies. As they saw others succeeding, their faith increased. As they personally succeeded, their faith increased more. Some people undoubtedly became deeply fearful or angry. But a combination of Koz's unfailing, visual, daily optimism and some short-term wins pushed enough employees over to excitement and pride. Enthusiasm, excitement, and pride spurred even more useful action—and voilà, a "miracle" occurred.

The Strategic Need for Speed

Speed is one of the most important strategic issues in a leap into the future. How fast must we go? How much time is minimally needed in each stage of the process? How much time must you allow for each wave of change?

Sometimes we just don't address these issues, leaving the pace of change to itself, unmanaged. Sometimes we are unrealistic about what can be done in a period of months, often because we under-estimate all the change that is necessary. Many times, after a few difficulties in steps 1 and 2, we talk ourselves into a very slow schedule to be "realistic." All these approaches to time can be dangerous.

More often than not, the question of speed is really very simple in today's world: The answer is to move as fast as possible.

The Body in the Living Room

From Ron Marshall

We had inertia. We needed change, and the pressures on us were building.

We could have layered this thing into a very deliberate, no rush-ing, three- or four-year process: One element of change in the first year, another in year two. This would reduce the amount of flux in the organization. Allowing for a four-year process gives people more time to adjust. We've all seen people who adjust slowly to change. Because a four-year process means less of a rush, maybe there will be fewer mistakes, and mistakes can be costly. What if you created too many short-term problems and lost the support of critical support-ers? You move a little slower and you have the time to give people a sense of involvement. You might be able to give them more of a sense of ownership. I could go on, but you get the picture—there are many pluses for rolling it out over four years.

There is a really good comment that a realtor made to me, years ago, when I bought my first house in New York. I leveraged like crazy to buy the house. It was a real stretch. After I closed, the realtor looked at me and said, "This is a fixer-upper, a real fixer-upper, a sixty-five-year-old house. Now, you've got to make sure that you make a list of all the things that you want to get fixed, and get it done in the first six months. Get it done in six months." I said "Are you out of your mind? A sixty-five-year-old house? I'm broke. By the time I pay the down payment, the taxes, your lawyer, my lawyer, I've got nothing left. Besides, I'm a disciplined guy. Over five years, I will be able to do what I want to do." She said, "No you won't, because after six months you get used to it. It seems to fit. You get used to stepping over the dead body in the living room."

I still remember this conversation. To my great surprise, she was right. I was wrong. Anything that didn't get fixed within six months didn't get fixed five years later when I sold the house.

Something like this can happen to companies too. A slow approach to achieving a vision can require an incredible amount of discipline inside a big fixer-upper. What can happen is that the organization just rolls a bit and then gets satisfied and stops. So if you don't act quickly, organizational inertia will overcome you. At the first sign of any success—after you've put out the fire in the oven and you've painted your fixer-upper—you're tempted to say, "Well, we took care of that." No more fixing up.

Another problem you can have with a strategy of slow change is related to the corrosive effect—that drip, drip, drip effect. There's a fear, an uncertainty, a doubt that comes into any change process. "Richard left; am I next?" And if that happens over four years, you have continual instability, which does not help.

I think this is a very big issue. You may have the vision, but it's crucial to think about how fast you want to move in achieving it. I guess there are times when slow is a good answer—when less pressure is on the organization, when the internal resistance might be overwhelming, when the enterprise is just too big, when you haven't a clue at first what to do. But that was not us.

We chose to move fast. In retrospect, it was an important choice.

Obviously, you can move too fast and find yourself in deep trouble, perhaps increasing fear and anger to dangerous levels.

This happens. But we should always remember that in a twenty-first-century world, the pace of external change is only going to increase. This will generally mean that the internal rate of change will have to increase too. If you wonder if that's possible, consider this: "The Videotape of the Angry Customer" (step 1) was done in a few days, "Gloves on the Boardroom Table" (step 1) in a month, "Painting Pictures of the Future" (step 2) in a few months, the crucial meeting in "General Mollo and I Were Floating in the Water" (step 2) in one hour, the crucial part of "The Plane Will Not Move!" (step 3) in a few weeks, and the vision in "Cost vs. Service" (step 3) in a month. In all these cases, someone with faith and optimism refused to say, "No, we can't move any faster because. . . ."

In "The Body," the selection of a move-quick strategy was informed by a memorable, vivid story. That story may have been told by Ron to his people many times. The image would have become one more element influencing the strategies they developed. You might think that influence would be trivial. What can a story do?

A good rule of thumb from examining human history, the role of parables, and the influence of the Christian Bible: Never underestimate the power of a good story.

An Exercise That Might Help

If a guiding team does not have a vision for their change effort, or does not have a vision they are satisfied with, try this.

Work with this group to draft an "article" for *Fortune* magazine about the results of their change effort, projecting five years into the future. In the article, talk about the following:

- How the organization is different

- What customers have to say about the company

- What employees are saying

- Performance on relevant indexes

In doing this, be concrete—include quotes from people, actual numbers, and a clear description of a new product or service or process.

In general, make it look like a real *Fortune* article.

You might have one meeting to capture the ideas, and then have someone write a rough draft of the piece. The draft would be sent out before a second meeting in which additions, edits, and so forth would be made. You would decide, depending on the particulars of your situation, how many sessions there should be and the length of the sessions.

Get the Vision Right

Create the right vision and strategies to guide action in all of the remaining stages of change.

WHAT WORKS

- Trying to see—literally—possible futures
- Visions that are so clear that they can be articulated in one minute or written up on one page
- Visions that are moving—such as a commitment to serving people
- Strategies that are bold enough to make bold visions a reality
- Paying careful attention to the strategic question of how quickly to introduce change

WHAT DOES NOT WORK

- Assuming that linear or logical plans and budgets alone adequately guide behavior when you're trying to leap into the future
- Overly analytic, financially based vision exercises
- Visions of slashing costs, which can be emotionally depressing and anxiety creating
- Giving people fifty-four logical reasons why they need to create strategies that are bolder than they have ever created before

STORIES TO REMEMBER

- Painting Pictures of the Future
- Cost versus Service
- The Plane Will Not Move!
- The Body in the Living Room

STEP 4

Communicate for Buy-In

STEP ONE
Increase Urgency

STEP TWO
Build the Guiding Team

STEP THREE
Get the Vision Right

STEP FOUR
Communicate for Buy-In

STEP FIVE
Empower Action

STEP SIX
Create Short-Term Wins

STEP SEVEN
Don't Let Up

STEP EIGHT
Make Change Stick

N SUCCESSFUL CHANGE EFFORTS, THE vision and strategies are not locked in a room with the guiding team. The direction of change is widely communicated, and communicated for both understanding and gut-level buy-in. The goal: to get as many people as possible acting to make the vision a reality.

Vision communication fails for many reasons. Perhaps the most obvious is lack of clarity. People wonder, "What are they talking about?" Usually, this lack of clarity means step 3 has been done poorly. Fuzzy or illogical visions and strategies cannot be communicated with clarity and sound logic. But, in addition, step 4 has its own set of distinct challenges that can undermine a transformation, even if the vision is perfect.

More Than Data Transfer

When we communicate about a large-scale change, common responses are: "I don't see why we need to change that much," "They don't know what they're doing," "We'll never be able to pull this off," "Are these guys serious or is this a part of some more complicated game I don't understand?" "Are they just trying to line their pockets at my expense?" and "Good heavens, what will happen to me?" In successful change efforts, a guiding team doesn't argue with this reality, declaring it unfair or illogical. They simply find ways to deal with it. The key is one basic insight: Good communication is not just data transfer. You need to show people something that addresses their anxieties, that accepts their anger, that is credible in a very gut-level sense, and that evokes faith in the vision. Great leaders do this well almost effortlessly. The rest of us usually need to do homework before we open our mouths.

Preparing for Q&A

From Mike Davies and Kevin Bygate

Three years after we initiated all the changes, everybody in the organization, from senior management on down, had a different job. Pulling that off without disrupting our customers was quite a trick. The basic communication about the new team-based organization was carried out by twenty managers, all of whom had helped develop the idea. Eventually, they talked to every worker and trade union. To help the twenty managers, we did a great deal of work, both on the presentation and the preparation for the Q&A. We thought a great deal about how the changes might affect people. Within the uncertainties and the timetables, there were limits to what we knew, but we pushed the limits. We wanted to be able to answer as many questions as possible of the "what does this mean to me" variety. Without that sort of Q&A, we felt it would be very difficult for our people to buy into the direction we were heading and to understand why the team-based strategy was right.

In preparing for the Q&A, we used role plays. The twenty presenters would be themselves and the rest of the management would play the workforce. We would ask every tough question we could think of. We would try to tear the presentation to bits. So some chap would make his pitch and a hand would shoot up and say, "If I've only got experience of forklift truck driving and none of this other stuff, does that mean I'm going to be made redundant? Are you going to throw me out?" And before you could do much with that, another person would say, "How are we going to decide who the new team leaders are? How will we know that the process is going to be fair? We have a union because once so much was not done in a fair way. Won't the union have to have a big role?" About the time your head was spinning, another would ask, with a suspicious look on his face, "I've heard this is nothing but a way to disguise cost cutting." The first time you tried to deal with all this you usually ended up looking like a fool, confusing everyone, including yourself, or causing a riot in the "workforce."

We created a question-and-answer back-up document for the presenters. It had some 200 questions that came up in the role plays. Each had an answer. For example, one of the questions was "What will happen to the existing management structure, in particular the plant supervisor's role?" Now, you could have talked for ten minutes trying to begin answering that question. The response in the document took less than thirty seconds. The idea was always to be as clear, simple, and accurate as possible.

Our twenty "communicators" practiced and practiced. They learned the responses, tried them out, and did more role plays until they felt comfortable with nearly anything that might come at them. Handling 200 issues well may sound like too much, but we did it. Remember that this was not like answering questions about beekeeping first, then about fixing a tire, then who knows what topic. Everything was about us and where we were headed. The clearer that is in your mind, the easier it is to remember the issues and answers, and the easier it is to respond in a way that can be communicated well.

In some cases it was just a matter of learning information you did not know. In many cases the problem was how best to respond with the information you had. Questions can come out as statements, not questions. They can be driven by a lot of feeling, not thought. You need to respond to the feeling in the right way. With practice, you can learn to do it. Our people did, and most of them were very effective, even though they were not communication specialists. They didn't get beat up. They walked away feeling successful, which they were.

Self-confidence was often the key issue. I think you can often tell in thirty seconds whether the person presenting information really believes in it, really understands what is going on. This makes the message more acceptable. For us it was critical that the workers and unions found it acceptable.

I can't believe that what we did is not applicable nearly everywhere. I think too many people wing it.

Some employees, upon hearing that there will be a merger, or that there is going to be a commitment to developing a revolutionary new product, or whatever, will cheer. "It's about time." Some will just need help in understanding. "I'm sure this is great— just say the vision again, I'm not sure if I get the third strategy." But most people will be nervous, even if they feel a sense of urgency to do something, even if they think the change drivers

Preparing for Q&A

Seeing

Employees are given a well-prepared presentation about the change effort and are encouraged to ask any questions. During Q&A, each presenter responds quickly and clearly, with conviction, and without becoming defensive. This shows people that the ideas are not muddled, that the presenters have faith in the vision, and that those answering the questions think the changes are good for employees.

Feeling

Fear, anger, distrust, and pessimism shrink. A feeling of relief grows. Optimism that the changes are good, and faith in the future, grow.

Changing

Employees start to buy into the change. They waste less time having angry or anxious discussions among themselves. When asked, they start to take steps to help make the change happen.

are okay, even if the vision is sensible. All sorts of insecurities bubble to the surface. People have a fear that softly whispers: "Will this hurt me?" In "Q&A," they dealt with this reality by creating a play of sorts that spoke to these feelings, that quieted them, that even generated some excitement and new hope for the future. The play came in two acts: presentation, then questions and answers. They wrote the play with the audience constantly in mind. Who are they, what do they need to know, how will they respond? They chose the actors. They rehearsed. The second act was ten times as difficult as the first, so they rehearsed with a simulated, tough audience. Only when the actors were comfortable did they put on the performances. Then:

- They showed the audience a capacity to respond quickly and clearly, suggesting that the change ideas were not muddled.

- The actors responded with conviction, suggesting that they had faith in what they were doing.

- They handled tough questions without becoming defensive, suggesting that they thought what they were doing was good for the enterprise and its employees.

Yes, the audience received information, but, more important, their feelings were addressed and modified. With that, minds opened to hear more clearly any direction for change, and energy developed for helping make it happen.

Cutting through the Avalanche of Information

Imagine a Q&A session, as carefully planned as in the previous story, being given only for twenty minutes at the end of a day-long meeting, a meeting that included four other discussions, nine speeches, and more. Sounds ridiculous, but we do the equivalent of that all the time.

Our channels of communication are overstuffed. Such is the nature of modern life. But most of the flood of information is irrelevant to us, or marginally relevant at best. An interesting (although disturbing) experiment would be to videotape your day, filming all the conversations, mail, e-mail, meetings, newspapers read, TV watched, and so forth. Then study the tape and see what percentage of that information you really need to do your job well. You'd have to do this with some sophistication because, for example, a seemingly irrelevant short conversation might be important because it builds a relationship with someone upon whom you depend. But still, the results of the experiment would be clear. You are hit daily with a fire hose blast of information, only a fraction of which is required to be an excellent employee. Believe it or not, "a fraction" could mean 1 percent. With clogged channels, even if someone is emotionally predisposed to want to understand a change vision, the information can become lost in the immense clutter.

Part of the solution has to be removing some of the clutter.

My Portal

From Fred Woods

One of the largest obstacles preventing meaningful change in our company is our inability to get important messages to our 120,000 employees. Our people get masses of communication, coming from all different areas. First there's a message about your 401k. Then there is a memo from your supervisor. Then there is a message from our IT director about internal information security.

Then maybe a brochure from a political action committee trying to raise money. All this arrives first thing in the morning, every morning. Sometimes I think people just get paralyzed and don't read any of it.

When I travel with Doug, our CEO, he'll inevitably get a question from an employee during a town hall meeting saying, "I didn't know about such-and-such," or "Why don't we talk more about blah, blah, blah?" And Doug's response is always, "There was a story in *Barron's* last week that was just about that" or "We talked about that three times in our staff meeting last month." Doug will then glare at me because he apparently feels I'm not doing my communications staff job. He thinks I'm not getting this information to them. But we *are* getting the information to employees. They just don't remember it because even if they read it ten days ago, they've had so much information since then they've forgotten. Or they got a huge pile and were paralyzed because they knew that in fifteen minutes six customers were going to be in front of them, so they dumped the whole pile in the wastebasket.

We're in the process of trying to change this.

Leadership needs to hold the primary responsibility for communication. There is no question there. It can't be assigned to a communications staff. But we can help them by clearing the channels. That's what we're now focused on.

We've looked at the nature of the communication that flows to employees. What we found was that 80 percent of what they got every day was being pushed out to them. They didn't ask for it, and they probably didn't need it. They just got it, like it or not.

To tackle this problem, we've taken a lesson from Yahoo.com. We are in the process of developing an employee Web site where we push out information every day for our employees. Using the My Yahoo! idea, we have started to develop what we are calling My Portal, which will let employees tailor the information they see on their desktop. From all the more routine stuff—and that's what I am talking about, the routine stuff—employees can get information concerning their specific needs in the workplace. And just that information—

nothing more unless they want more. They'll get information that is easy for them to understand, information that they either act upon that day or can put away until they need it.

Once it's up and running, My Portal will be a huge step in lightening the flood of routine communication landing on employees and make it easier for us to get the big, important, nonroutine messages out. We don't have precise measures, but all the initial feedback we have says people are very excited about the potential of getting much less irrelevant stuff and designing a tool that will allow them to better understand the important issues. Not only will My Portal help the firm, I think people will really appreciate our efforts to lighten their load.

My Portal is far from a panacea. But it's an interesting use of new technologies to reduce the information clutter. It will run into resistance. "What?" says the marketing, personnel, or finance bureaucrat, "Everyone *must* know this information about X. It must be sent to them!" You have to deal with situations like this, where people cling to the old ways of communicating. But remember, without a clear channel, you can't influence feelings and create needed behavior.

The unclogging concept is a good one and can be applied in many places. With today's technology, why should everyone get the same company newspaper crammed mostly with information of low relevance? We already know that instead of receiving 100 pages of your local city's newspaper, you can get 2 pages from the Internet each day on topics of relevance to your life. If that's possible, why not in an organization? In a similar vein, why should large numbers of people be stuck in meetings of marginal importance? We all hate this. It adds to information overload (and to our anger). All this was a problem in a slowly changing world. With a much faster-paced world, the problem grows greatly.

Matching Words and Deeds

People in change-successful enterprises do a much better job than most in eliminating the destructive gap between words and deeds.

Deeds speak volumes. When you say one thing and then do another, cynical feelings can grow exponentially. Conversely, walking the talk can be most powerful. You say that the whole culture is going to change to be more participatory, and then for the first time ever you change the annual management meeting so that participants have real conversations, not endless talking heads with short, trivial Q&A periods. You speak of a vision of innovation, and then turn the people who come up with good new ideas into heroes. You talk globalization and immediately appoint two foreigners to senior management. You emphasize cost cutting and start with eliminating the extravagance surrounding the executive staff.

Nuking the Executive Floor

From Laura Tennison

When we presented our vision of the future, I thought we were getting acceptance, and some enthusiasm. But then I began hearing that a few employees thought it was outrageous that we talked about being a low-cost producer while our executive offices were so grand. They said, in effect, "How can you be serious about improving productivity when you are wasting so many resources maintaining such an elaborate executive area?" In my judgment, they were right. And the more they talked, the more other people began to think the same thing.

The executive floor in our headquarters building was a world unto itself. The rooms were huge. The joke was that you could play a half-court basketball game in the chairman's office. Almost every office included an adjoining conference room and private bath. Many of the bathrooms had showers. There was enough polished wood all around to build a very nice ship. There was a private express elevator going to that floor. There was an elaborate security system that required a staff of at least four people. There was expensive art on the walls. It was incredible.

All of this had some reason for being. We once didn't pay that well, and the offices were a big part of the attraction for wanting to be in top management. Big clients once upon a time often judged whether they should do business with us by the prosperity (or lack thereof) shown in the executive area. The security was put in after some unpleasant incidents in the 1970s.

We had discussions about how to deal with the problem. We could take out the bathrooms except the one in the chairman's office. Maybe we could turn a few of the conference rooms into offices. Or maybe take the most expensive art and give it on loan to the museum. But the discussions went nowhere. "These ideas will cost more money. We're trying to save money." "We've got big competitive issues, why are we worrying about furniture?"

Two years ago we got a new CEO. I remember wondering if he would do anything about the executive offices. I didn't have to wonder long.

Almost immediately after taking the job he nuked the entire floor. We tore everything down to the outside walls and rebuilt. People were relocated on another floor while the construction was in process. Offices were reduced in size. The bathrooms disappeared. We put in plenty of conference rooms, but not one per office. The new décor is lighter, looks more contemporary, and was not nearly as expensive as the old mahogany. We added more technology and reduced the number of secretaries. We converted the express elevator to a local one, used by all. We sold the art. We also made the security less noticeable and less labor intensive.

I think just the announcement that we were going to do all this had a powerful effect. When people saw the end result, and lived with it every time they visited that floor, the effect built. You can't believe how different the executive area looked and felt. The rich men's club was completely gone.

The one criticism of this was that all the construction was an additional expense. But we could show that by adding offices, reducing secretaries, selling art, reducing security costs, making it easier for employees to move around the building (because of the freed-up elevator), we could pay for the changes in twenty-four months, and after that operating costs would be significantly lower. I'm not sure how many people know that, or care much. They just care that the executives seem to be better at walking the talk.

For at least three reasons, matching words and deeds is usually tough, even for a dedicated guiding team. First, you sometimes don't even notice the mismatch. "What does the size of the offices have to with the real issues: duplication of effort, too many levels of bureaucracy, a sloppy procurement process?" Second, you see the mismatch but underestimate its importance and then spend too little time seeking a solution. "Redoing the floor will cost more money. There is no way to get around that reality." Third, you see the answer but don't like it (a smaller office, no bathroom!).

In highly successful change efforts, members of the guiding team help each other with this problem. At the end of their meetings, they might ask, "Have our actions in the past week been consistent with the change vision?" When the answer is no, as it almost always is, they go on to ask, "What do we do now and how can we avoid the same mistake in the future?" With a sense of urgency, an emotional commitment to others on the guiding team, and a deep belief in the vision, change leaders will make personal sacrifices.

Honest communication can help greatly with all but the most cynical of employees. The guiding team says, "We too are being asked to change. We, like you, won't get it right immediately. That means there will be seeming inconsistencies between what we say and do. We need your help and support, just as we will do everything to give you our help and support."

By and large, people love honesty. It makes them feel safer. They often love honesty even when the message is not necessarily what they would most like to hear.

New Technologies

Great vision communication usually means heartfelt messages are coming from real human beings. But new technologies, as cold and inhuman as they are, can offer useful channels for sending information. These channels include satellite broadcasts, teleconferencing, Webcasts, and e-mail.

Although a satellite picture of the boss is not the same as having him in the same room, it can be a lot better than a memo. Even a videotaped interaction with the boss and some employees can show others more than information on paper.

New technology can solve communication problems very creatively. For example, one problem is that messages come and go. The president is in the room, but then she leaves. The memo is good, but it eventually goes in the trash. So what doesn't leave the room? What could stay day and night, beaming a message on and on?

The Screen Saver

From Ken Moran

There was no set screen saver before we introduced this. Everyone chose their own—some sort of wallpaper, something they downloaded from the Internet. Your normal morning went something like this: You walk into the office, get your coffee, greet your coworkers, go to your desk, log on to the computer . . . and your day begins.

Now imagine walking in, getting your coffee, greeting friends, logging on, and discovering that something is different. You take a closer look at your computer screen and realize that the picture of fish that usually greets you every morning has been replaced with a multicolored map of the UK surrounded by a bright blue circle. As the image slowly moves around your screen, you read the words surrounding the circle: "We will be #1 in the UK market by 2001." This was exactly the image we presented to all employees one morning about two years ago.

Because the screen savers appeared on all computers the same morning, we surprised everyone. We had recently announced our new vision, so the concept wasn't new. The point was not to introduce the vision in this way, but to show our commitment to it and to keep it fresh in people's minds. The aspiration to become number one is pretty infinite. We wanted people to know that this was not just another fad, or just a warm and fuzzy hope. This was an absolute, a constant. By putting the message on people's computers so that they saw the logo every time they logged on, we found a simple way to continually reinforce our message.

Needless to say, the arrival of the screen savers had everyone talking. That day, you'd hear people in the halls saying, "The strangest thing happened when I logged on this morning . . . Oh, you got one of those new screen savers too? Did everyone get one? What's this all about?" Over the next few weeks, the conversation moved toward "Do you think we can become number one by 2001?" At a later department meeting, they might talk about new metrics: having five new products in the UK by 2001, growing at a rate of at least 15 percent a year, and being number one in sales each year. "If we hit those targets," people said, "I think we'll definitely achieve the vision."

Of course there were the skeptics who didn't appreciate the fact that we had removed "their" screen saver. They probably felt like we were forcing this down their throats. On the day the screen savers arrived, their conversations were more like, "How dare they change my computer! What happened to my old screen saver?" These were the people who had a problem accepting the fact that they would have to change, so it wasn't really the screen saver that was the issue. These were the people who wanted to ignore our new vision, to write it off as just another fad and wait for the initiative to go away. The new screen saver and the conversations it sparked, on top of all the other communications circulating around the company, made it very difficult to ignore our vision.

After a while, we updated the computer image to include other metrics. We still had the UK map surrounded in the blue circle, but we changed the message around it. This sparked new conversations about our goals and our vision. I could walk around the office and ask people what last year's results were and what this year's target was and many could respond without even having to think about it. These were people that, a year before, might not have even been able to quote the company's vision, let alone its targets.

We continued to update the screen saver, and it's become a sort of corporate icon around here. It's great because, instead of a newsletter or flyer that's here today and gone tomorrow, it is a constant reminder of our company's goals. It's amazing what can happen if large numbers of us all understand what the goals are.

Done poorly, a new and unexpected screen saver could seem like Big Brother in the most Orwellian sense. But look what they were able to do here.

The visual image is an important part of this method. People read, yes, but they also see, with all the power of seeing. Other new technologies offer similar benefits. The satellite broadcasts a moving picture. The teleconference with an executive people know sends more than voice—an audience can conjure up an image in their minds. A video over the intranet is like the satellite broadcast. We will be seeing increasing video over the Internet, even though the words could come much cheaper as text.

As with the issue of urgency (step 1), none of these methods are remotely sufficient by themselves. You generate a gut-level buy-in with Webcasts and a screen saver in conjunction with well-prepared Q&A sessions, new architecture, and more. At times, you might think all the communication absorbs an inordinate amount of time and resources. But it's all relative. If we have been raised in an era of incremental change, with little vision and strategy communication required, then what is needed now can seem, quite logically, like a burden. Yet most of the burden is in up-to-speed costs. Learn new skills, unclog the channels, add the new technology, and it is no longer a tall mountain to climb. It becomes just another part of organizational life that helps create a great future.

An Exercise That Might Help

The goal is to assess accurately how well those around you understand and have bought into a change vision and strategies.

Method 1

Find a group of individuals who employees see as "safe." Perhaps Human Resource people who have good relations with the workforce or consultants who swear confidentiality and look credible. Have them talk to a representative sample of employees in your organizational unit (always focus where you have influence). The questions are: "We need to know how well we have communicated the change vision and strategies. What is your understanding? Are they sensible? Do they seem compelling? Do you (really) want to help?" The interviewers can aggregate the information without naming names and give it to you. This need not be expensive, even in a large organization. That's the beauty of sampling.

Method 2

If your enterprise already polls employees each year with an "attitude study" or the like, add some items related to the communication issue. "Do you understand the change vision? Do you buy into it?" This method is very cheap and easy, but you must wait until the yearly cycle.

Method 3

Construct a special questionnaire and send it to employees. You can ask more questions than in method 2, and do it when you want, but it will cost more and draw more attention.

> More attention is both good and bad. If you are feeling frag-
> ile and risk averse, for whatever reasons, forget it.
>
> ### Method 4
>
> Just talk to people informally about the issues. Listen to the
> words, yes, but also pay attention to the underlying feelings.

Communicate for Buy-In

Communicate change visions and strategies effectively so as to create both understanding and a gut-level buy-in.

WHAT WORKS

- Keeping communication simple and heartfelt, not complex and technocratic
- Doing your homework before communicating, especially to understand what people are *feeling*
- Speaking to anxieties, confusion, anger, and distrust
- Ridding communication channels of junk so that important messages can go through
- Using new technologies to help people see the vision (intranet, satellites, etc.)

WHAT DOES NOT WORK

- Undercommunicating, which happens all the time
- Speaking as though you are only transferring information
- Accidentally fostering cynicism by not walking the talk

STORIES TO REMEMBER

- Preparing for Q&A
- My Portal
- Nuking the Executive Floor
- The Screen Saver

STEP 5

Empower Action

STEP ONE
Increase Urgency

STEP TWO
Build the Guiding Team

STEP THREE
Get the Vision Right

STEP FOUR
Communicate for Buy-In

STEP FIVE
Empower Action

STEP SIX
Create Short-Term Wins

STEP SEVEN
Don't Let Up

STEP EIGHT
Make Change Stick

I N HIGHLY SUCCESSFUL CHANGE EFFORTS, when people begin to understand and act on a change vision, you remove barriers in their paths. You take away the tattered sails and give them better ones. You take a wind in their faces and create a wind at their backs. You take away a pessimistic skipper and give the crew an optimistic boss.

The word *empowerment* comes with so much baggage, you might be tempted to abandon it. We won't. As we use the term, empowerment is not about giving people new authority and new responsibilities and then walking away. It is all about removing barriers.

Removing the "Boss" Barrier

Often the single biggest obstacle is a boss—an immediate manager or someone higher in the hierarchy, a first-line supervisor or an executive vice president. Subordinates see the vision and want to help, but are effectively shut down. The supervisor's words, actions, or even subtle vibrations say "This change is stupid." The underlings, not being fools, either give up or spend an inordinate amount of time trying to maneuver around the barrier.

The "boss barrier" is typically handled in one of three ways. We ignore the issue, we send the obstacle to a short training course, or (rarely) we try to fire, demote, or transfer the person. None of these are great solutions, the first for obvious reasons, the second because it usually has little effect, and the third because, if not handled well, fear will escalate and become a disempowering force itself.

In cases of highly successful change, people begin by confronting the issue. In order to be fair, they explain the situation to the individual creating the problem. When explaining fails, as it often does, they try more creative solutions.

Retooling the Boss

From Tim Wallace

There was one superintendent in our company, Joe, who was considered so "old school" that people had warned me he would never change his ways. He had been with the company for over twenty years and he was very proud of our products. Whenever a customer would want a change in the product or how we made it, this man would get bent out of shape. He felt we were giving people a great product and that they were too picky. When someone would suggest something, he would respond in one of two ways: We tried it and it didn't work, or we thought about it and decided not to try it. It seemed to me he was basically a good man, a talented man, and a man with a lot of valuable experience who was stuck in an old paradigm. He just couldn't see anything from the customer's point of view.

Once, it became so tense that one of our best customers said that we needed to replace Joe. I didn't like the idea of terminating an employee who probably thought he was protecting the company. So I thought about it and then said to the customer, "Let's do something different which might help both of us."

We asked them if Joe could go to work for their company for six months at our expense. He would work at a different place and have a different boss. To help make this happen, we agreed to keep paying his salary. We further said that after six months we would bring him back into our company as a customer representative, inspecting our products specifically for that customer. This would be a different job than he had before, but an important job. The idea was to convert the guy from being an obstacle for others into someone who would actively help us.

Joe's boss thought the plan wouldn't work—may have even thought it was nuts—but he agreed to go along with it. Joe was at first also very reluctant to accept the idea. "I have my own job to do and I don't want to do something else." I told him we really needed his expertise so that he could tell us what was going on when our tankers arrived at the customer's facility. But he was a real hard rock. He didn't want any part of this plan. So we had his boss tell him that he couldn't have his existing job anymore, that he could take our offer or leave.

Off he went into a different world. His new job was to be a quality inspector at the customer's plant. I don't know how difficult it was on him at first, but he had to change to survive. He had to learn a new job, a new company, and how to look at our products from that customer's point of view. If he didn't, he failed.

Well, he didn't want to fail, so he tried to do the new job. And when he started really looking, he found that an old product of ours, which he thought was very good, didn't meet the customer's needs. He found that they bought this product because they didn't have an alternative and switching would be costly. He found that another product, which he also thought was very high-quality, was not seen by the customer that way because of how they needed to use it. And he found that our delivery on another product created additional problems.

So then he came back to us saying "This is no good. You don't understand that by doing this, you are hurting the customer. We've got to change or we risk losing their business."

Joe ended up being the best inspector the customer had ever had. They loved him. When he came back to us he was a new man. The "old school" barrier, the change resistor, became one of our best managers.

I suppose there are many people that you can't do much with, or people that you can't afford the expense of doing much with. But I think you need to be very careful when you hear people saying that so-and-so is hopeless. It might be true, or it might not.

Our jobs determine a large part of what we see each and every day. The experience of changing a job can be powerful. False pride and a feeling that all's well can be blown away. For a fragile and very insecure person, without lots of support, fear could escalate and the person could be immobilized. But for many people, the experience can be life changing—from being stuck in the past to leaping into the future. For the organization the experience can be most helpful—in this case, a disempowering manager became one who empowers.

For those on top, the entire middle management will occasionally seem like a barrier. They're "the rock in the middle." Senior

Retooling the Boss

Seeing

With a new temporary job working as a parts inspector for a customer, a man is confronted with the quality problems his group has been creating. He sees the problems hour after hour, day after day.

Feeling

Pushed into the job, the man is at first mad and perhaps scared. After a few days in his new position, he is surprised and shocked by what he finds.

Changing, Seeing, Feeling, Changing

He starts trying to identify and solve the quality problems. He sees the results and sees how the customer reacts. The positive reaction and results reduce anger and fear and induce more positive feelings in him. He tries harder to solve the problems, sees the results, and a useful see-feel-change cycle develops. When he returns to his regular employer, his behavior is significantly different. He no longer makes it difficult or impossible for his people to help the change effort. Just the opposite—he becomes an empowering change leader.

management wants to get on with the change (sometimes an over-statement) and so do many employees, but the rock is in the way. The big question is: Why is the disempowering rock such a rock? Listen to the answers so often given: "They're tied to the past." "They can't learn a new style." "They are protecting their jobs." Well, yes, but these answers are pessimistic and condescending. Look deeper, and more often than not, you'll find a different or more fundamental reason for the existence of the rock. The reason: Steps 1 through 4 did not successfully address middle management, or the steps were not undertaken at all. So without the presence of sufficient urgency, sufficient faith in the people leading change, or in the change vision, what would you do, especially if most of your peers felt the same? Wouldn't you join the Rock Club?

Removing the "System" Barrier

A second, very common source of disempowerment is the formal set of arrangements we often call *the system*. A decade or two ago, this would have mostly been overwhelming bureaucracy—layers in the hierarchy, rules, and procedures—which ties the hands of employees who want to help make a vision a reality. Generic bureaucracy is still an issue, especially in the public sector, but today the performance evaluation and rewards part of the system is often the stickiest problem.

Evaluation and rewards can disempower when they are at odds with the direction of needed change. The new vision and strategies say x, but the bureaucracy not only does little to identify and reward x, it helps block what is needed. "We want you to boldly leap into the future" is the communication, yet the system says "Boldly leap into the future and you will receive ten cents if you succeed and a hammer on the head if you fail." Conversely, evaluation and rewards can empower people by identifying and compensating behavior that is required by the vision.

The Worldwide Competition

From Louise Berringer

We wanted to make big advances, real breakthroughs, not 20 percent but 50 percent better. We knew this was possible, but we also knew that, because of our history, most employees wouldn't agree. They'd say "We have had trouble doing 10 percent." We needed to *show* them that this was possible, to help them see that they were capable of greater achievements. That's how the worldwide competition was invented.

We decided that if we wanted dramatic improvements we should have a dramatic recognition program, something very different than what we had been doing. This worldwide competition we created allows team entrants from any part of our operation, in any country. Once the team registers, they start working on their "improvement idea" and are judged against other teams at the local level. The winners move to the next stage and are compared to other teams at the regional level. Then they move on to a global competition.

The finals are always hosted somewhere special, not here at headquarters in Frankfurt. This year we did Bali. We were in a large conference room for a day and a half in a really nice hotel. There were ten teams from around the world. The judging was done by some of our top management along with representatives from a few of our customers. The overall attendance for the event was about a hundred people.

Each team had to do their presentation in English. That's one of the rules. For some of these people it's really hard. They don't speak a lot of English and it might have been the first time they have ever traveled outside their country. We once had a team from India who had never even been outside their own village.

They each have twenty minutes. We are very strict about that. If a team goes over the twenty-minute slot, we sound a hooter and they have to stop. That way we can keep the presentations to a manageable amount of time, and the people in the audience can give their full attention to each one.

The teams this year were very innovative with how they used the twenty minutes. One group had a panel with characters from their home country and they made their presentation into a quiz show. The "host" would ask the questions. "Can one of the panel please tell me the name of the tool that reduced our cycle time by 50 percent?" Then the buzzers would go off and lights would be flashing and someone would answer. They were all dressed up, pretending to be panelists with their name tags hanging on the front of the podium. That might sound ridiculous, but it was a great way to present what they had done. Another team pretended they were in a normal meeting back at their home base, sitting around a table discussing the issue and coming up with the solution to the problem. As they talked about their solution the rest of the audience learned what they had done. Many teams brought samples of their product with them—anything from the tiniest CD player to a large electronic piano—just to show what they were talking about.

We gave all of the teams the afternoon to have fun. Then we all came together again in the evening for the final presentations and some serious celebration. We had local dancers, stalls with things people could buy, a sit-down dinner outside in the hotel's gardens with traditional island food. I think everyone was wearing a grass skirt over their regular clothes! It built up to the end. The music started playing. I think it was "We Are the Champions." The runners-up were announced. Each of them received a certificate. All the other teams clapped like mad! And then we announced the winners. "Simply the Best" was playing at full volume as they came up on stage.

The Spanish team's project was judged to be the very best from a terrific group of entries. A trophy was presented to the team leader, and each of the six members received a medal. They were standing there in shirts made up of their national colors and all of these big guys were crying. It was incredibly moving.

We've been doing it for three years. The first year we had 300 teams with an average of seven people on each. About 2,000 people were involved. Last year we had 875 teams. We have just closed off registration for this year with 1,400 teams entered (representing about 9,000 people).

It is amazing what these groups have achieved and are achieving, and the influence they are having on nearly everyone in the company. We have concrete results from the teams in the competition. We have communication about the 50 percent breakthroughs and the effect they are having on the business. And not only that, but we see others in the organization who in the past would never have taken up an issue, now rising to the challenge. In some cases they violate a lot of the standard procedures we have in the company. They break the rules. We see people who work in manufacturing or production start developing new products. This is quite far removed from what they should be doing, but they see a fault, they see a way to make it better, and they get on and do it regardless of past practices or organization charts. People feel empowered to do this.

When we think of evaluation and rewards, most of us think of money. In this day and age, few people believe they have more cash than they need. Many, many households struggle, even with two incomes. Thus, when there are no economic rewards for transformation, you can have a barrier that can be very powerful. But the addition of bonuses and raises does not necessarily motivate a change in behavior, nor does it necessarily convince people that the downside of failure will go unpunished by the system.

In "Worldwide Competition," we have a different sort of evaluation and reward. Evaluation is not done by a single boss or by some set of impersonal measures. Proof of performance is not supplied only by reports. Rewards are not cash in the pocket. Instead, once again, we have carefully staged dramas. There is the country-level drama, then one at the regional level, and the biggest one at the global level. Each is full of memorable sights—the city, the elaborate ceremony, the costumes, the visual and emotional presentations. The awards ceremony takes this all over the top. The dramas touch the feelings deeply, then become vivid stories that are told and retold to others not in attendance at the events. And the moral of the stories, at least in an organization not overwhelmed with cynics, is pretty clear: The company wants you to leap, will cheer when you leap, and cares deeply when you leap. As the stories are told and retold, they can hit a chord and behavior really changes.

Competitions can be cheap manipulations designed to avoid paying for performance. But people are not stupid. They can spot a cheap manipulation. Then cynicism and anger grow and grow. Sincerity is crucial and, in many ways, quite easy for a committed guiding team who believe in a vision.

Removing Barriers in the Mind

In "Worldwide Competition," we also see one of the greatest disempowering barriers of all: the mind. After years of stability, incremental change, or failed attempts at change, people can internalize a deep belief that they are not capable of achieving a leap. They may not say out loud "I can't do it," but at some level they feel it, even when it is not true.

We've all seen this. "No," thinks the sixty-year-old. "I'll never be able to learn to use the computer." Yet there is nothing about his or her IQ, manual skills, or ability to hold information in memory that blocks action. The problem is, as we say, "all in the head," that is, psychological and irrational.

A good rule of thumb: Never underestimate the power of the mind to disempower. Another rule: Never underestimate the power of clever people to help others see the possibilities, to help them generate a feeling of faith, and to change behavior.

I Survived, So You Can Too

From Greg Hughes and Dalene McCann

I remember back in the early days, when we had just finished forming teams throughout the organization. We had created twenty-one of them in total—not a small task in itself—in order to look at how to improve service across our different departments. Well, whenever you form teams, especially many of them, there is all this turmoil. There is uncertainty about what is going on, uncertainty about the size of the task facing everyone, uncertainty about the overall direction. This discomfort started to coalesce into doubt that the vision could really be achieved. Maybe it was too grand, too much at once, not the right thing for our particular department, etc.

Ron, getting wind of this growing doubt and anxiety, hauls all 200 of us into a meeting. He pulls out chart after chart after chart of the process changes they made at Lexmark, his former employer. Changes to how they dealt with their customers. Changes to how they provided internal services such as HR. He went on and on. Pretty soon what we were undertaking started to look pretty easy compared to what they had done.

Then he hit us with the videos. At Lexmark, they had filmed the order-taking process before and after the change. Before, people were basically glorified message takers. Afterward, they were customer relationship managers. They had the tools and skills to provide product promises and delivery commitments right on the phone. They could deal with service problems themselves, directly. Both the level of service provided and the service providers themselves had been transformed. They also filmed people talking about their hopes and vision for the future before the change and then their exuberance actually living the vision in the new organization.

We watched and people believed. Ron's previous experience, demonstrated so concretely, was a jolt of new energy. By the end of the meeting, people were buzzing again. "If Lexmark could cut the time it takes to finalize a contract from a month to three days, maybe we can do the same with the time it takes us to issue hunting permits or fishing permits or whatever other permits that currently take us two months to issue. It's not too far-fetched. Ron did it, Lexmark did it; why can't we do it?"

That was the beginning. A rocky start, but hey, we're sailing now, right? Well, not quite. I was sitting in on a meeting with the warehouse people and this raging debate breaks out that looks destined to end in an all-out, knock 'em dead brawl. The team was kind of segregated between old and new. There were employees who had been with the organization about two years and there was another group that had been with the organization about thirty years. They were like oil and water. The young guys had totally bought into the vision. They were saying that we need to tear down everything we are doing today and build a greenfield site. We need to clean-sheet everything. We need to close down warehouses. Change is great; let's go. Now on the other side of the table are sitting our thirty-year veterans who were integral in building what these young folks were proposing to tear down, and they were saying, "The hell you will." Tempers were rising fast and it was getting ugly.

The young consultant who was on the team and trying to manage this meeting went high-tailing it out of the room and did what was probably the smartest move of his career. He got Ron. So Ron enters the room and the furor subsides slightly. And he says, "We are going to change the process fundamentally"—and all the young guys are nodding—"but we're not going to close twenty-two district warehouses. We're not going to fire 6,000 people. We're going to find another way." Now this had been said before, but the old guard weren't feeling like this was possible. Ron says, "At Lexmark, through our reengineering effort, we were able to reduce our working capital. We were able to reduce the amount of inventory we kept. But we didn't close the warehouse; we reduced the cost of carrying the inventory. For example, we got our auto parts supplier to deliver the parts on demand so we didn't have to keep our own store of them.

We freed up a lot of space in our warehouses, but we didn't go and close them all. We didn't fire a bunch of people, but we did save a good deal of money. You can do the same types of things here." That kind of calmed them down. But there was nothing I could have said that would have helped. I hadn't been through it before. He had. The number of times he saved us, I can only guess.

I think you need to understand that you are not first, that others have survived these changes. It gives you more confidence. Even after you have agreed with the overall idea, it helps you get past the little voices in your head that get in the way. It gets you beyond "Yeah, but this can't possibly work" or "This will only work if I die in the process." Seeing someone else's survival makes you feel stronger.

I suppose if you have gone through successful change of some magnitude, you will have people who know what is possible and have self-confidence. This was not our case. External resources brought us hope, experience, and the utter conviction that we could make a difference. Whether by design or pure chance, outsiders were interspersed throughout the organization, maybe creating some resentment at first but overcoming that with all they added. Not just Ron. Aldona Valicenti came from Amoco. Patrice Carroll was a newcomer to our part of the organization. These people, in addition to the outside consultants, helped add something important. Again and again when things seemed to be descending into chaos and the brink of collapse, they added stability. They reassured us and kept us on course. They were our rock of Gibraltar—our prophets of things to come. Each of the newcomers brought with them a wealth of experience and reassurances that change of this magnitude had happened before and succeeded. Their perspective was really critical.

Without conviction that you can make change happen, you will not act, even if you see the vision. Your feelings will hold you back.

At one level, this story offers a simple, yet powerful tactic. If your people do not have experience with significant successful change, make sure you find credible sources and have them constantly available. Some consultants make a living from this. Of course, there is the risk that if you do it poorly, the newcomers will be squashed by the culture, and the consultants will be ignored. But that need not happen.

Credible sources can help in a number of ways. They can present data. "We have found in seven cases in the past four years that $235,000 was saved, on average, and the firms without change experience saved nearly as much as the others." Done well, this can help. Solid logic can also help. "The method by which we saved the money is based on the theory that. . . ." But look at the core of what happened in "I Survived." You had "turmoil," "anxiety," "discomfort," "rage," and "tempers." You had "feelings" that the changes were not possible. People dealt successfully with these emotions by telling many vivid stories and playing many videos about actual events. The key content was rather simple: "This is possible; you won't die in the process; the end result can be very important." And what happened? The negative feelings shrunk, and the positives grew. "We watched and we believed." We received "a jolt of new energy." The disempowering mind barriers were reduced, and they moved on with the changes.

Removing Information Barriers

Information is a source of power, and a lack of information disempowers. That was a part of the problem in "Retooling" (a lack of information on customer needs), "Worldwide Competition" (information on how 50 percent improvements are possible), and "I Survived" (information on successful change efforts).

One of the most powerful forms of information is feedback on our own actions. We are often remarkably unaware of how we spend our time, how we interact with others, and how we physically move about. When we do get feedback, it comes from another person, often sounding and feeling subjective, biased, or like a precursor to sanctions. So we end up with little valid information, or information that seems suspect. In either case, we have more difficulty achieving a vision. It need not be that way.

Making Movies on the Factory Floor

From Rick Simmons

For years, senior management came and "inspected things" at the plant. The plant manager only received instructions about what needed to be improved. "Fix that. This is no good. Don't do that." It was never anything positive, just what we needed to fix. Well, on one of these visits, Tim, our division executive, said that because of our new change effort, there would be no more plant inspections. He said we had to "empower" the workforce. That's how we were going to really get better. It couldn't be done by senior management because they didn't have the time or the information.

We tried to work it out. But it was like "ready, fire, aim" in the worst sense. It was chaos. Empowerment meant involvement, so we instituted employee improvement meetings, and for six months we had meeting after meeting. But people really didn't know what to do. After a while, the meetings started to deteriorate into bitching sessions. "We can't get the right inventory numbers because the reports are always one month behind, so what's the use of these reports? They're just no good." "Why are we always having breakdowns in our welding equipment? If we had more equipment we wouldn't have this problem." "If corporate would just provide more direction, we wouldn't be mired in this mess." "Do you realize how much time we are putting into these meetings?" Fewer people turned up to the team meetings, and the ones who came started

saying, "What's the point, it's not going to make any difference anyway." The meetings became really unpleasant to attend. We finally
realized that they were doing no good, so we decided to try something completely different. But our overall empowerment goal
remained unchanged.

We took two of the teams who we knew were fairly open to trying new things, and we started to film them at work. They agreed
with this—it wasn't anything sneaky. It just seemed like a better way
of understanding how we currently operated. Tim had provided us
with a handheld camcorder and video equipment, but until that
point the teams hadn't done anything with them.

We started off by just following how one product was manufac-
tured. It was a really lengthy process. We captured on film everything
from the guy grabbing the raw material off a shelf to the last person
taking the finished product off the line and preparing to ship it.
There were pictures of Tyron setting up the tanker skin for welding,
Claude doing the actual welding, and then Sam pressure testing the
strength of the welds. There was some awkwardness and jokes at
first. "I hear the camera adds twenty pounds." For a while people
were more careful and unnatural about what they were doing than
usual. But after we filmed someone doing the same activities several
times, they tended to go about their tasks oblivious to our presence.
It probably took us about a day of filming to get one stage of production really nailed down. The outcome was amazing.

When we sat down and watched the tape, you could see that
people were having to walk literally miles around the plant to get this
one piece of equipment finished. When we brought in the team that
we had filmed and they viewed the tape, the ideas started flowing
automatically. They talked about how we could reorganize where
the machines were so that we could cut down how far people had to
walk. They looked at themselves on tape and saw that they were
having to go to a store cupboard every time they needed a new tool
to use. Just watching the tape, you would hear people saying to
themselves, "Now why don't I just have a rack with all the tools I

need next to me?" "Look at how many times I'm bending over to pick up the ratchet wrench to tighten a bolt." "Maybe if we had someone sort out the repair equipment and materials we use to complete a machine repair, we could pick the stuff up at the loading dock rather than coming to the supply room and pick it up ourselves. If we did this, I bet we could do the job faster."

The teams started to rethink options that would make the work easier and safer. One of the team members even hand whittled out of wood two sets of our machinery. He then arranged them to show how the machines had been set up before and then how they had been reorganized to reduce walking time. It really gave us a three-dimensional picture of the change. This helped us explain the concept to other teams and to customers who were brought to the plant by Tim and the sales people. Nobody asked this guy to create these models of the plant. He just thought it would help.

All of the improvements that people came up with had to be evaluated through a typical business case exercise before the OK was given, so people couldn't just do anything they wanted. But the filming became a very important tool for the workforce. It helped to spawn good ideas that they could put forward.

The videos themselves have continued to be used. We have kept them as a historical archive of the types of changes we have put in place. After the first round of filming, we started to make the videos more professional. We now have literally hundreds of taped examples of how we used to do a certain part of the job and then what we did to improve it. We keep track of the cost savings or safety and quality improvements this has brought about. We now show new employees and visitors these tapes. That helps us get people on board and helps us improve our relationships with customers. And you definitely get a sense of the pride the teams have when they present their improvements.

We also refashioned the site meeting room so that more people could fit into it to watch the tapes and discuss ideas for improvement. That meeting room has become a bit of a showpiece and a focal point for people to get together. All the tapes documenting the changes that the plant has been through are stored in there. And it started with a camcorder that cost less than 1 percent of some of the machines in the plant.

Their first attempt to empower the workforce failed, and failed in a very common way: Employees were given more decision-making power; they were put in meetings in order to exercise that power; but they were given few guidelines, and few tools for eliminating real barriers. The mess that follows is predictable.

In their second attempt, they used a camera to help empower a work group with feedback. The movies surprised people, so they paid attention. They saw, for the first time, aspects of their actions of which they were unaware. And so the possibilities for making their work lives better jumped out, creating for many an excitement and a we-can-do-better optimism. Those feelings led to more useful changes, including the carving of the wooden models. The models then became another visual mechanism to help alter still more behavior. When the changes worked well, people saw this, pride blossomed, and the virtuous cycle continued.

Not Doing Everything at Once

People successfully empower others when they understand the idea. They empower because they correctly see what the key obstacles are and what is keeping them in place. They empower by mustering courage and self-confidence within themselves.

People act cowardly, or at least seem to, for many reasons. Perhaps most of all, they hold back because the obstacles blocking action can seem gargantuan. They have a boss problem, an entire middle management problem, a reward system problem, an information system problem, a mind problem, and more. All these challenges can seem overwhelming because, in total, they *are* overwhelming.

You don't have to be crushed, no matter how complex the situation. There is a solution, and it's simple: Don't try to do everything at once.

Harold and Lidia

From Jeff Collins

We have two people in our San Francisco office, Harold and Lidia, who sat down with me last year (I'm in corporate HR) to look at barriers in their department to a big new-product development concept they have. We had flip chart paper all over the walls. Many of the problems, like the corporate compensation system, were totally out of their control. So we crossed those off. From the rest, they chose two issues to work on. The first related to engineering team leaders, people in their own department, who brutally beat on new ideas. The second was a lack of any formal process for capturing new-product brainstorms.

They hauled ten people from the department off-site (the group has about twenty or thirty people in total). At the meeting, they talked about what they were collectively doing to stomp on new ideas and they agreed to help each other stop this. They didn't try to work on their bosses; they focused on themselves. They also outlined a mechanism that could allow people to speak up more and offer product ideas. It isn't much more sophisticated than a suggestion box system. But it's a system.

When they returned from their meeting, the ten of them continued to work on the two issues. Changing their own style was a challenge, especially for four members of the group. Some of those not at the meeting reacted with suspicion or total disinterest in the suggestion system. Nevertheless, over the following two or three months, ten new ideas were generated, one of which was very promising. So they were off and running.

I think this simple story is so important because of what they didn't do. They didn't choose fifteen issues to work on. I don't know if I were in their place that I wouldn't have done fifteen. They played it much more pragmatically, and more focused. So far, that has worked extremely well. They are creating a radically different new-product development process out on the West Coast, and all indications are that it will soon give birth to a big product prototype. Given our track record over the last decade, that's a big deal for us.

Empower Action

Deal effectively with obstacles that block action, especially disempowering bosses, lack of information, the wrong performance measurement and reward systems, and lack of self-confidence.

WHAT WORKS

- Finding individuals with change experience who can bolster people's self-confidence with we-won-you-can-too anecdotes
- Recognition and reward systems that inspire, promote optimism, and build self-confidence
- Feedback that can help people make better vision-related decisions
- "Retooling" disempowering managers by giving them new jobs that clearly show the need for change.

WHAT DOES NOT WORK

- Ignoring bosses who seriously disempower their subordinates
- Solving the boss problem by taking away their power (making them mad and scared) and giving it to their subordinates
- Trying to remove all the barriers at once
- Giving in to your own pessimism and fears

STORIES TO REMEMBER

- Retooling the Boss
- The Worldwide Competition
- I Survived, So You Can Too
- Making Movies on the Factory Floor
- Harold and Lidia

STEP 6

Create Short-Term Wins

STEP ONE
Increase Urgency

STEP TWO
Build the Guiding Team

STEP THREE
Get the Vision Right

STEP FOUR
Communicate for Buy-In

STEP FIVE
Empower Action

STEP SIX
Create Short-Term Wins

STEP SEVEN
Don't Let Up

STEP EIGHT
Make Change Stick

I N SUCCESSFUL CHANGE EFFORTS, empowered people create short-term wins—victories that nourish faith in the change effort, emotionally reward the hard workers, keep the critics at bay, and build momentum. Without sufficient wins that are visible, timely, unambiguous, and meaningful to others, change efforts inevitably run into serious problems.

The Nature and Function of Short-Term Wins

George has a laser-like focus on a potentially lucrative e-business concept. He leads a team that has dozens of people empowered to pursue various projects, and most of those people are doing so with enthusiasm. From his vantage point, the whole process is incredibly exciting, sometimes scary, and never boring. Twelve months into the effort, he is convinced all is on track, that they have made extraordinary progress under the circumstances. Others who are less enthusiastic begin to raise more and more questions about the initiative. "Yes, this is important, but why are you doing such and such?" "Yes, this is interesting, but isn't it interfering too much with our current business?" "Yes, but didn't we try that two years ago and fail?"

Dealing with these questions is distracting, takes time and energy, and ultimately becomes maddening. Every time he thinks he has presented an argument that puts an issue to rest, someone revives it, often with more energy, not less. "Yes, but now I'm really worried about. . . ." He articulates the vision again and again but finds that some people only want to have what seem like metaphysical conversations. He sees these people increasingly as cave dwellers, as creatures who will sooner or later kill the organization, leaving it in the dust. He isolates his staff, putting others in the role of attackers, a role that they increasingly accept. Eventually, key supporters withdraw, and the whole effort is overrun with what seem like infidels. An important and promising set of ideas dies an undistinguished death.

Cary has the same one-year budget and a different, equally powerful, e-business idea. Twelve months into the effort, her group is seemingly behind George's team. They have fewer projects exploring fewer ideas. They are not as able to fill a report or a meeting with interesting words. But Cary's people have an up-and-running Web site, a site that is fully developed for one small and carefully targeted customer segment. This small subprototype begins receiving daily customer feedback that looks promising by any standard. Excitement within her group and support from others grow. As George sinks into the mud, Cary begins to soar. George can't believe her good luck and wonders if her short-term outlook is one more sign that his company is in trouble.

George is a smart and dedicated man. But he doesn't get it.

In successful change efforts, an empowered group of people are very selective in how they spend their time. They focus first on tasks where they can quickly achieve unambiguous, visible, and meaningful achievements. These short-term wins are essential, serving four important purposes:

1. Wins provide feedback to change leaders about the validity of their visions and strategies.

2. Wins give those working hard to achieve a vision a pat on the back, an emotional uplift.

3. Wins build faith in the effort, attracting those who are not yet actively helping.

4. Wins take power away from cynics.

Without these achievements, large-scale change rarely happens, and the infidels do seem to take over, regardless of how brilliant the vision and how needed the changes. But with these accomplishments, you find the opposite: a growing sense of optimism, of energy, and of belief in change.

Focus Is Essential

Because of the very nature of large-scale change, much must be done to achieve the vision. In sizable organizations, a change effort might ultimately require hundreds of projects. When people feel urgency and are empowered to act, they can easily charge ahead on all fronts. With scattered attention, you might find the first unambiguous wins in two years. Two years is too late.

The List on the Bulletin Boards

From Ross Kao

We have learned that when an organization has a great many things to do to correct its course, those leading the change are tempted to put 150 balls in the air all at one time. There is so much to do, you certainly can find 150 balls to put into play. Everyone can come up with a long list of things. But with so much going on at once, you run the danger of getting nothing finished very fast. This creates problems. It leads to frustration. People wonder where you're leading them—and whether or not you're taking the right approach.

To avoid that, we created something called "the Big Four." We knew what our priorities were. We could have listed the top twenty, but we didn't. Instead, we went public with just four goals. In essence, we said to the entire organization, "These are the top four things that we're working on. And until we get one substantially completed, we're not adding number five."

We literally published: "Here are the top four." At every work site we located large bulletin boards that everyone frequented and posted these top four items. In a factory, the board was in the canteen. It quickly became a device for saying, "Look! We're going to go do something. We're going to get it done. And guess what? Everybody look! It's done. And look, we just added another one to the list. And oh, by the way, this one is going to be done in another two weeks." The next thing you know, people are saying, "You know what? Things are happening. Things *are* getting done."

I remember I was out in the factory and I happened to be standing beside the Big Four list. This guy from the line came by and looked at the list with me. After about half a minute he turns to me and he says, "We're really knocking 'em down." People knew it. They felt the energy.

Now, granted, there were some people running around the organization saying, "You mean what I've been doing isn't important?"

"No," we'd say, "that isn't what we mean. We're just telling you that that's not what we're working on right now. You need to know that what we're going to do is get something done with lightning speed. We're going to get it completed, and we're going to make sure we've got enough energy and collective participation to get this thing implemented before we move on to the next item."

For an organization that had been treading water, creating and communicating our quick wins really helped us begin to gather momentum.

Four instead of 150 means focus. Focus means more is achieved quickly. Quick achievements provide so much: a feeling of accomplishment, a sense of optimism. With this, behavior changes. Those who have worked so hard to create the wins are reenergized. Those who have been pessimistically or skeptically sitting on the sidelines begin to help. Cynics make less disruptive noise. So momentum grows.

Bulletin boards are misused all the time. Put them off to the side where people do not congregate. Clutter the boards with fifty pieces of paper. Put up propaganda ("We're all committed to the vision!"). Make vague statements ("We're making progress"). Not in this story.

The Power of Visible, Unambiguous, and Meaningful Wins

Not all wins are equal. In general, the more visible victories are, the more they help the change process. What you don't know about is not a win—hence, the potential usefulness of a cafeteria bulletin board. The more unambiguous the wins are, the more they help the change process. With less ambiguity, fewer people will argue about whether a success is a success—so power is taken from the cynics. The more the wins speak to employee issues, concerns, and values, the more they help the process. Valued achievements connect to people at a deeper level—and a deeper level can change behavior that is generally very difficult to change.

Creating the New Navy

From Rear Admiral John Totushek

The U.S. Navy has relied upon its Naval Reserve since 1915. The reserve force has consisted of civilians, many of whom are former military members. They train on weekends and work with the active force two weeks each year. They are there to serve in times of war or national emergency.

Historically, the two forces have been managed separately. Now, due to a number of events that began with the collapse of the Soviet Union, our views on our organizations are changing. The active Navy can no longer afford as many full-time regular personnel, which means that they need to rely more and more upon our reserve force. We cannot afford unnecessary duplication of resources. As a result, we have developed a new vision for the Navy and the Naval Reserve—and are creating a new structure in which we are pulling the management of two large organizations closer together. It is both a management challenge and a cultural challenge.

For many years, certainly up until Operation Desert Storm in 1991, reservists were silently acknowledged by some in the active Navy as "just reservists." They were to be called upon to replenish the active force when it needed more manpower. The active duty forces saw themselves as the ones doing the "real work" of keeping ships and aircraft ready for combat and carrying out operational missions. The reservists were considered "only" a force in waiting. In many commands, active forces would provide work for reservists, but would keep a close, even wary, eye on their "part-time" brethren. In some commands, attitudes developed about not trusting reserve force members with real authority or real responsibility. Yet, with the past decade's shrinking active force, more responsibility inevitably and necessarily shifted to the reserves, and to the surprise of some of the old guard, the reserves succeeded beyond all expectations. Roles were changing, yet even as we entered the post–Cold War world, old attitudes persisted in the active Navy. These attitudes made it more difficult to pull the two organizations into one Navy.

As we have been trying to change those perceptions, we have been working hard to create successes that would show both the active and reserve forces how interdependence with one another can benefit both—and meld us into one force. We began by discussing goals that were attainable and desirable.

I remember a commander during one of those sessions suggesting that we develop a new curriculum for Officer Candidate School that would focus on educating the active force about the reserve force, and vice versa. The curriculum would focus on our being One Navy. We thought it would be fairly easy to change the curriculum and get our message into the hands of our new officers. If we achieved this, we would achieve something with a long-term, far-reaching impact. We all agreed that getting such a curriculum in place would be a great "win" and would certainly help reinforce our vision in each succeeding generation of sailors. Then someone said, "Yes, but if I am already on active duty, or I am a reservist, how meaningful is this new curriculum to me? And is it really that visible a change? How will it help us win over the hundreds of thousands of active and reserve officers and enlisted sailors we already have out there? I realize it should be done, but I'm not sure that it characterizes a good short-term win."

That comment started us thinking, and from there, we more clearly defined characteristics of our short-term wins. In order to gain support out in the field, we needed successes that on the one hand were visible and on the other meaningful. This would make the wins really hit home. So we literally looked at everything we might do.

Then we pinpointed which activities met our criteria and tried to create a timeline that would produce a continuous stream of successes.

For example: If we were to be one force, we needed to do a much better job of matching the skills among reserve personnel with the continually growing needs of the active Navy. Until recently, this was a long, tedious, manpower-intensive process. It didn't always produce the desired results within the required time frames. Finding a readily available reservist with public affairs skills and Korean language proficiency, or an information technology specialist with expertise in information security, often meant relying on word of mouth. You can imagine what a difficult task that is in two very large and distinct organizations.

We decided we could record our Naval Reservists' civilian and military skills into a useful, interactive, flexible, Web-based database. Authorized Navy personnel could quickly search for certain types of skills. There would be some individual privacy requirements, but we thought we could address these issues. Here was a project that would be meaningful to many people. It would be visible to many people. And it would be inexpensive and easily implemented because we could adapt architecture that was developed, funded, and already in use by another Defense Department agency.

Reservists, using password protection, can now directly post and update their education and civilian skills, including language and equipment proficiencies, and personal contact information. Authorized active Navy personnel can tap into the Web site and describe their request. They view online reports describing the skills, experience, and qualifications of persons who fit the profile, but not names and contact information. Active Navy personnel can then e-mail our Naval Reserve Command in New Orleans, which will act as intermediary for matching up the requirement with the available reservist. The system isn't perfect, but it is visible to many people and is seen as useful to many.

Our successes are helping people in both forces believe in what we are trying to accomplish. In a little over thirty days, I received messages from the active Navy admirals in charge of the Pacific Fleet, Mediterranean and North Atlantic areas, and the Naval Air Forces in the Mediterranean. Their messages were uniformly positive. Bit by bit, we are showing our officers and enlisted sailors that we are serious about having One Navy. We're showing them that the vision of a One Navy Force is working and that it is not just talk.

If you have been a part of enough successful change efforts, you will understand the power of visible, meaningful, and unambiguous wins. If you have not, you can miss the mark. Too often we create wins that *we* see, but which others do not, at least not to the same degree. Visiting an office in Japan, we see a breakthrough in a cancer drug using a new method of drug development. We find the victory and are able to ask questions and poke around. We conclude it is a big win and we leave pumped. Our colleagues in New Jersey read about the experiment and are excited, but not nearly as much without actually seeing the animals, talking to the researchers, and feeling the energy in the office. Too often we create wins that are meaningful to *us,* but much less so to others. We have enormously strong feelings about cancer, and though the key research personnel in New Jersey share these feelings to a degree, their hearts are invested much more in the problem of antiseizure agents. So while we are deeply moved by the Japanese wins, many of our colleagues in New Jersey are not. "Oh yes," they say in a very rational manner, "this is important." But they don't rush to understand the development process that created the breakthrough. They don't change their behavior. And that's a problem.

In "New Navy," a group very deliberately tried to avoid this problem by (1) clarifying the criteria for a good short-term win and (2) selecting projects based on that criteria. The educational program could have been helpful, but not as much as a resource-finding system that was highly visible and that was generally more valued than education. The results of a curriculum change could have been evaluated, but the Web site provided much more measurable outcomes.

Choosing What to Target First

The order of projects can also make an important difference in large-scale change efforts. You can choose what to target first based on a logic that seems eminently rational but which does not supply enough wins fast enough to build necessary momentum. Suppose the vision is globalization. One choice that seems rational is to work on the manufacturing piece before the marketing. Make it before you sell it. Focus first on building a plant in Frankfurt. But building the Frankfurt factory might easily take two years, a hundred million dollars, and then another year to assess whether the firm can handle its first German manufacturing facility. During this time, unambiguous, visible, meaningful wins would be hard to find. A less obvious but better choice is, in a sense, to sell a product, then make it. Put together a marketing plan for Germany. Implement the plan at minimum cost with a product from Chicago. Achieve a first clear success in less than a year.

In choosing well what to target first, you must satisfy the most basic criteria: achieving visible, meaningful, and unambiguous progress quickly. Beyond that, relatively easy options are obviously attractive—it is cheap and fast to open a Frankfurt office versus expensive and slow to build a plant. The easiest of the easy are often called "low-hanging fruit." Less obvious to many people, but also important, are possibilities that focus on a powerful person or group whose help you need.

The Senator Owned a Trucking Company

From Ron Bingham

One of our state senators owns a trucking company. He's an important person whose support could make a difference to our change effort. I thought, to help us start building momentum, what can we do for trucking companies?

I went to talk to him and it turns out that he is really mad that the state makes him fill out fifteen forms a year, some of them very long. "Do you know how much time and effort this takes?" He has his secretary dig around and find the forms. "Look at this!" he says. He doesn't quite wave things in my face, but that's the idea.

I look at the forms and my first impression is that this is bureaucracy at its worst. "The same information is asked here and here and here." He says it politely, but I think he would like to strangle someone. "When I fill out some of these, I have to get three or four people involved." I can easily imagine that. "We want to run a company that has jobs and customers. We don't want to fill out unnecessary forms."

I went and met with our change team in the transportation department. They had been struggling a bit to get cooperation with a lot of senior people in the department. You see, in government—at least in old government—there was often a "I'll wait you out" kind of approach. Basically, if you stall long enough, the governor will change and the program that has been irritating you will go away. Well, the transportation group had been running into this, so they were ready for suggestions. I met with them and told them what the senator had told me. I said, "You guys need to put fixing these forms on the top of your agenda." They didn't agree right away. They basically said, "Jeez, Ron, we've got all these great and big things we need to get completed here and you're trying to sell us on changing a few forms. That hardly seems like the grand change vision we had pictured." I understood where they were coming from. They had all this energy. They wanted to change the world. But they weren't getting anywhere because key constituents like the senator weren't helping them. I explained how getting this win for the senator, while taking time up front, would actually give them more credibility and support to do the things that were really important to them. So somewhat grudgingly they started down the path of redesigning the licensing process. It took maybe a month to get done. And they did an amazing job.

For all those who say "What can you do with government, it's just inherently a mess," they should listen to this. A vision of less bureaucracy, more efficiency, and better service to the public is not unrealistic. The transportation team reduced the paperwork from fifteen forms to one. And they didn't lose any key information, didn't undermine any needed government function. That's the sort of change that is possible, the sort of change that so many people inside and outside the government didn't think was possible. That's the sort of change that if you thought it wasn't feasible, you wouldn't waste time and resources trying to help someone who did.

When we were done, I took this back to the senator and showed it to him. "Damn, you guys are really doing something," he says. Before that he had heard briefings on our work, but it was all talk. Now he could see it. It wasn't just talk about another change project. And he could feel it because it affected something that was important to him. After that, the senator was one of our biggest supporters.

We have had several of these short-term successes, and now people believe in us and our work. The resistance has gone down, and the successes have helped make it real for the team. They don't have to wait three years to feel like they are making a difference.

In selecting where to focus first, a key criterion applied in "The Senator" was to assist a powerful person as soon as possible.

The assistance can alter the person's feelings about the change effort, which can increase his or her support of that effort. This behavior change can produce more subsequent wins than if a less powerful person were helped.

The application of this principle can lead to a very different starting point than a more linear, "logical" model. The application of this principle can seem less "efficient" than some other possibilities. But who needs a fuel-efficient car if the driver becomes bored, stops, and never arrives at the finish line?

And If We Can't Produce . . .

In some cases, all sorts of factors can block us from producing powerful enough wins at a pace that is needed. How we deal with this reality can be very important. When the wins are not there, the temptation, the oh-so-great temptation, is to stretch the truth, to exaggerate a bit. Not to lie, of course—we'd never lie. We just put the best possible light on events. Right?

Hoopla

From Dave Pariseau

We have been working to introduce a new IT system and new ways of working across our major operating divisions. This has been one of the largest changes our company has undertaken and it's been painful at times. Twenty-four months into the effort, it was not obvious to most people whether this was working. They felt pain but little gain. It was not at all clear to top management what the financial paybacks were. Those leading the change were under a lot of pressure to produce some tangible successes, some wins to show people who were suffering that we were on the right track.

The core project team started sending a weekly e-mail to everyone in the company called "Message of the Week." It was a status update. I can remember one that said "90 percent of our pre-go-live objectives have been met. Nearly all of our people have been trained and they are prepared and ready to do their jobs." Well, there were a lot of employees who just didn't agree with that message. The people who would be using the new system, who might have been trained on how to use the new software, were nearly all saying they had no real idea about how their jobs would change when the machine was switched on. Many of the project teams who were based on each site, and who were much closer to the way the business worked than the core project team, totally disagreed that 90 percent of the work was done.

Every communication we received was pretty much the same. As time went on, if anything, it got worse. Message of the Week seemed to have turned into project propaganda. One message said that a division had been making great strides with the new system and work processes, that they had improved their efficiency by something like an incredible 500 percent. It would make you think we had won World War III! But I remember some of the people from my division who were in regular contact with those in the "500 percent improvement division." Our people said they only heard complaining.

It was like this everywhere. People were finding it really hard to adjust to the new software. They would read these communications and be thinking, "This is a nightmare. We haven't won World War III; we're going down! What are they talking about?"

It got so bad that even when Message of the Week told of real successes, things that we really had achieved as a result of all of the effort, the credibility of the communication had become so low that people ignored the message. I'm trying to remember a "good" piece of news that I actually believed in, and I can't! This is despite the fact that I have been committed for the past three years to seeing the change effort be successful.

> Part of this may be our culture. We seem to be more comfortable communicating "sunshine and roses." You know: "Be honest, but positive whenever you send a message like this out." But more than that, when the good results just didn't happen, we started to feel a bit desperate in the face of some criticism. So we overplayed the positives to such an extent that they became unbelievable, regardless of whether they were real or imagined. So the skepticism grew, and this was really bad.
>
> I suspect that any form of hoopla is a mistake.

From this account, we don't know exactly why they had no short-term wins. Perhaps they didn't pay sufficient attention to the issue. Perhaps the early steps in the change process were not done well, making the wins task much more difficult. Whatever the case, they found themselves in a box and then did what is so tempting—stretching the truth. Possibly they were stretching the truth in their own minds, and not in any sense lying. Possibly they did not understand clearly that wins must be unambiguous. The result was disastrous. When their credibility collapsed, even a legitimate win was viewed with suspicion.

The best solution to the "Hoopla" problem is to never get into a position where it seems necessary to stretch the truth. The better you understand the issues in this chapter, in the entire book, the better the odds that you won't. The second-best solution is never to try to exaggerate your way out of the box. Honesty always trumps propaganda. And honesty starts with being truthful with ourselves.

Being honest with yourself isn't a bad strategy for all the steps in large-scale change.

An Exercise That Might Help

Make a list of projects or tasks that could be tackled by empowered people within the organization in which you have influence—projects or tasks that could be short-term wins.

1. For each item on the list, assess the following:

   - When could you realistically get this done? How many months?

   - How much effort and expense will it take? Grade it on a 1 to 10 scale, from almost no effort to huge time and expense.

   - How unambiguous will the win be? Try another 1 to 10 scale.

   - How visible will it be? (1 to 10)

   - Will this be viewed as a meaningful win? (1 to 10)

   - Who will see it as meaningful? How powerful are these people?

2. Given these assessments, which of the items on your list should receive priority?

   - Pick the top five.

   - What's number one?

Create Short-Term Wins

Produce sufficient short-term wins, sufficiently fast, to energize the change helpers, enlighten the pessimists, defuse the cynics, and build momentum for the effort.

WHAT WORKS

- Early wins that come fast
- Wins that are as visible as possible to as many people as possible
- Wins that penetrate emotional defenses by being unambiguous
- Wins that are meaningful to others—the more deeply meaningful the better
- Early wins that speak to powerful players whose support you need and do not yet have
- Wins that can be achieved cheaply and easily, even if they seem small compared with the grand vision

WHAT DOES NOT WORK

- Launching fifty projects all at once
- Providing the first win too slowly
- Stretching the truth

STORIES TO REMEMBER

- The List on the Bulletin Boards
- Creating the New Navy
- The Senator Owned a Trucking Company
- Hoopla

STEP 7

Don't Let Up

AFTER THE FIRST SET OF SHORT-term wins, a change effort will have direction and momentum. In successful situations, people build on this momentum to make a vision a reality by keeping urgency up and a feeling of false pride down; by eliminating unnecessary, exhausting, and demoralizing work; and by not declaring victory prematurely.

143

Keeping Urgency Up

The most common problem at this stage in change efforts is sagging urgency. Success becomes an albatross. "We've won," people say, and you have problems reminiscent of those in step 1.

PE Ratios

From Leonard Schaeffer

When we began, nearly everyone in the company was motivated to change because of the threat of being closed down. Then, as we started to turn ourselves around, there was a lot of excitement throughout the organization. People were motivated by our recent success and challenged by the new challenges. As we made more and more changes, we kept the momentum from slowing by comparing ourselves to similar healthcare companies. We explored our strengths and weaknesses along a number of dimensions in each of our business divisions. On top of that, I was out there talking face to face with all the people in our organization once a month. I would try to explain why we were making the changes and talk about the metrics that we were trying to achieve and the competitors we faced. There was Q&A. As we grew larger, we used teleconferencing once a month to get the same messages out.

When we started to lead the field, comparing ourselves to our competitors became a piece of cake. If anything, we kept reconfirming the fact that we were miles ahead of everyone. In light of this success, we were faced with the tendency to fall into complacency. After all, things were good; we were at the top of the mountain. What was the reason to keep on renewing ourselves, to keep on building the stronger organization that would inevitably be needed in the future? People began to say, "But we *are* number one." Even worse for me, "Why won't the boss just let up?"

This was no good. But what could I do?

Now we've started using the idea of looking at ourselves "from the investor's point of view." What that means is that we've started to compare where we are in relation to other investment opportunities within the broad healthcare field. The real message now is: We're in competition not just with firms like us but also for investor's dollars. This is no longer about just us and how well we run our business. This is no longer just about our success in relation to the competition out there creating the exact same products and services as we do. This is about recognizing the fact that other people are out there in the healthcare industry doing some pretty amazing things. Those people are getting a lot of attention and a lot of money from investors. So we may be the best at what we do, but if another company can create a price to earnings [PE] ratio of 50 and our PE is 12, boy, we've got trouble.

The reaction to this new focus has been very interesting. With some effort at helping people understand this idea, a lot of them got a renewed sense of urgency pretty quickly. They started to see the loss of potential investors as a threat and they started thinking about ways we can improve our own position. They began recognizing that there are a lot of newer companies who are beginning to offer some of the same services we do.

There are some people, however, who still say, "Company X is in the business of doing Net-based software, so it's not a good comparison. People are investing in those companies for different reasons. They're attracted to the technology, or to the newness of the company. We can't compare ourselves to them." Maybe it's just human to want to think this way: They aren't relevant, so we're fine. I've been learning that you can never overcommunicate in helping people deal with these sorts of things. You have to be there talking with them as much as possible.

To keep you moving, in many situations it's going to be essential to have an external problem. If you are just going to beat up on people and say we have to do better, it doesn't work. People don't really believe you and it's not at all productive. Making more money doesn't do it either. There has to be something real that they can see outside that leads them to say "We haven't made ourselves into the

> organization we should be. We need to do more. We need to try harder. I'm willing to try harder."

It's easy for those driving change to allow urgency in the organization to drop when short-term performance rises. It's easy then to become frustrated and to "beat up" on your people. It's easy to declare victory too soon and become complacent yourself. This happens all the time. These traps are inherent in the very nature of large-scale change.

In "PE Ratios," Schaeffer tried to deal with the urgency problem by shifting people's frame of reference, how they looked at the situation. He used a new external comparison. How well such an approach works depends mostly on whether it changes how people feel about what they see. When they are tired, an intellectualized discussion of statistics can be twisted to fit complacent thinking. "Well yes, but what about . . . ?" Their reaction can be very different if they see a boss, in face-to-face communication, show his sincere belief in the new frame and show urgency based on that belief. Their reaction can be different if anyone else with credibility does the same—mutual fund managers, customers, and so on.

Almost all the step 1 methods can, with appropriate modifications, be used here. Imagine a firm having produced wave after wave of change, having its bottom line explode upward, having most employees and managers saying "You can't do better than this," and yet having many areas where the transformation has not even started—areas like purchasing. Then this guy has a college student do a little study about how many different kinds of gloves the firm buys. . . .

Tackling More and More Difficult Changes

Early in a change effort, you generally take on some of the easier problems in order to establish a few wins and create momentum.

Picking up every piece of furniture in a house at once and moving the giant mass across the street is not necessary or feasible. There aren't enough movers. We might not have anyone who wants to help with the 600-pound sofa. In a successful move, the lighter pieces—the wall pictures and small side tables—usually go first. But sooner or later, we are faced with the sofa and the bed and the credenza. Ultimately, all the basic pieces that we need for our new home must be moved, put in the right places, and made to work together correctly. If we forget one picture that isn't really relevant to our new décor, who cares? If we forget the refrigerator, we have a problem. If we put the stove on the wrong side of the kitchen, it's very annoying. Put the stove in the attic, and we have a mess.

Simple courage and perseverance help. Better still, structure situations so that people can take risks to deal with difficult bureaucratic and political problems without having to put their lives on the line. Structure situations so that people can gain the power to take on the most intractable problem. *Power* here means not just authority. More important can be time, resources, and access.

The Merchant of Fear

From Phil Nolan and Steve Featherstone

Our company has a horrible track record of investment planning. It has been going on long enough that it's become totally ingrained in the culture. Despite all the other changes we had made, this was something that we ignored, even though it was clear that we needed to deal with it to make the change effort really successful. We made excuses simply because the planning process cut across organizational units and the politics had become a huge barrier. So investments were not always made sensibly. "I can't do my job unless I have this budget and these projects." Well no, that's not true, but who wants to confront the problem if it's a powerful person and he's not the only person doing this. Push a little, and people dig in their heels. In an organization with a silo mentality, people often have little incentive to find a better way or to cooperate with each other.

This is where our "Action Labs" come into play. Action Labs are cross-company project teams that are given an unusual amount of leeway and power. Members of an Action Lab work full-time for a few months. So it's very intense. They have the right to talk to anybody they want, do anything they want, and operate with very few boundaries. They typically bond and listen more carefully to each other. So the person from one part of the organization starts to understand another part for the first time. They also become very candid with one another. As a group, they become more daring than any individual. With our encouragement, they start pursuing problems, start looking for solutions, in a way that just wouldn't normally happen on the job. We give them permission to be very creative and bold. Not all do so, but in some cases it's marvelous.

Our last lab was set up to focus squarely on the investment planning problem. Eight people were taken off their jobs and put on this full time for six weeks. They talked to the CEO and the executive group, the heads of some of our business divisions, those people who reported to them, the people who planned the budgets and did all the analysis, even the employees who type up the numbers and who have to keep adjusting the figures.

One thing the investment planning team did was to make a video that made fun of how people behaved when they put a budget together. It was a lighthearted way of getting a very serious message across. The video was a skit with characters like the Merchant of Fear, the Glory Hunter, and the People Protector. All were over-the-top spoofs of the types of behaviors that existed. Like all good spoofs, they hit the issues dead-on.

The Merchant of Fear would increase his own budget by drawing out and working off of people's fears. He would say things like "We had better keep a bit of reserve in my budget—just in case." If you ever tried to tackle a Merchant of Fear, he would have at least ten good reasons why he needed that amount of money to avoid having the company's network explode and kill one billion people, maybe more. "We need to budget for these five things. Actually, now I think about it, we'd also better add these two extra things too because what would happen if it were a building that went up? In fact, while we're at it, we might as well add these other thirty eventualities just in case we blow up an entire town." And it wouldn't matter that two of the budgeted items would have been enough. He would always have an answer as to why he needed more.

The Glory Hunter chased the high-profile management initiatives that could bring him fame and fortune. He focused on whatever was sexy at the time. He'd go after an important consulting project that had just been started or a key task force led by the CEO. He'd love a major engineering project where he could introduce new technology that would guarantee him a place in the company's historical archives or his picture on the wall. He would not share credit or do what was necessarily in the best interests of the company. He would just demand budgets for what made him look good.

The People Protector didn't want glory and wouldn't necessarily pander to fears. His sole objective was to make sure that there were enough projects for his staff. If these could match their skill sets and happen near their home base, then all the better. Regardless of what work was actually needed, the People Protector would just calculate how many projects would be required for his 200 people over eight months and then set his budget accordingly.

The Action Lab team showed the video of these characters to the top twenty or thirty executives, the very people who were being spoofed in the film. You can imagine the reaction! There was total shock. Immediately everyone was trying to guess who the characters had been based on in real life. Somebody even asked, "Is that meant to be me?" Something like this would never have been done in the past, never been remotely considered. Yet with the labs and the support from the CEO, it happened.

I think top management burned the film. But it worked. They still occasionally refer back to the characters. "Watch out, this is beginning to look like Merchant-of-Fear talk." It helped stop the old investment planning game in its tracks by exposing the types of behavior that went against the new, more shareholder-oriented vision.

We have found that not everyone works well in an Action Lab environment. You need people who are willing. You can't coerce people into doing something like this. They also have to have the technical knowledge or base of experience to work on the problem. They need to be willing to challenge the status quo for good reasons, to ask "why," and to question the rules instead of just accepting that something is set in stone because it's always been done that way. And they need to be able to leave their desk with the agreement that they won't be back until the lab is over. This last point is a real challenge. The types of people we need in Action Labs are typically not those who are easy to free up.

We have done ten of these labs. Not all have been great. The ones that have not worked so well did not have a clear focus or objective at the start. We've found if the groups do not work well because of the people dynamics, you have to make a decision there and then if it's salvageable or not and go with it. But most labs have been very useful, and their actions have made a difference.

One of our biggest regrets with the last lab is that we didn't find a way to make a copy of that video before it was burned!

Somewhere in the waves of change, you will have to attack the sturdy silos and difficult politics or you won't create a twenty-first-century organization. In the early stages of a transformation, the silos and politics can be too tough to handle. But eventually, you must choose to deal with this heavy lifting or you will never fulfill the vision.

In "The Merchant," the company made progress not because of task forces per se. They made progress because they set up conditions that gave a group sufficient power to blast through the barriers and complete another needed wave of change. Oddly, the group was a task force—oddly, because we don't think of task forces as powerful. But look at how they did it. First, the Action Labs groups were given great leeway. These sorts of cross-organization task forces often fail because they are put on short leashes. Second, the members were given sufficient time. Typically, people on these types of task forces are supposed to do the work in addition to their regular jobs. Third, they were given the opportunity to gather a broad range of data. There was no "Well, yes, but the chairman is out those three weeks." Fourth, they were not handed a conservative charter. There was no "Don't stir the waters too much; be practical; make sure any ideas can be implemented," the latter often a code phrase meaning "Make sure the ideas are so trivial that no one will try to block them." Because there were none of these constraints, it helped give people, after easier waves of change were completed, the power to attack the particularly difficult challenges.

Also key in the success of the "Merchant" task force was its creativity. Write a play showing the problems. Hire actors and film it. Make it funny—to diffuse some of the defensiveness and to reduce the frontal attack on a norm of underlings not criticizing the bosses, perhaps even a norm of no heavy conflict allowed in public. If the fun came across as angry and ridiculing, the risk would have been much higher. But it didn't. If the problems spoofed were not the spot-on real problems, a defensive person could trash the film. But apparently the task force did a good job of putting its finger right on the issues. If no one on the executive committee was frustrated by the destructive behavior, the top management could still have found a way to rationalize the "stupid" film and ignore it. But that was not the case here, and probably never is. The film gave those who were frustrated, a group that is often larger than is apparent, a legitimate tool, and a feeling of optimism, to try to eliminate unhealthy behavior. In combination with other actions—and other actions would have been necessary—the wall started to fall, and the change process had a chance of making it all the way to the end.

Images can be powerful. Even if viewed only once, they can stick in the mind for a long time. A month later, someone could refer to "The Merchant of Fear" video and the idea (and feeling) would still be there because a strong image was instilled. That seems to be the way the mind works.

Not Killing Ourselves

Deep into a transformation, even if urgency remains high, even if people want to take on the big problems, and even if they succeed in generating waves of change, they can still fail because of exhaustion. They find they have to keep the organization running, which means doing all the old work. On top of that they have to handle additional work to create the future. So people are overwhelmed and eventually start to resent it. For many individuals, the situation can feel as if there is no solution—which isn't true.

In successful transformations the answer is, at one level, very simple: When you have too much work, jettison some.

Reducing Twenty-Five Pages to Two

From Ken Moran and Rick Browning

After the teams had been functioning for a while, and the change process seemed to be working, we began getting a ton of feedback about how we were creating too much pressure on people in terms of workload. They were taking their day-to-day work home on the weekends. "Ken, my wife is complaining." "Ken, this is no good, we can't keep this up." "Ken, if I call the local paper, send them to your office, then walk in and die, this will not help your career."

An e-mail went out to people saying that this was *not* incremental work. This was not "Do your job and add all this new activity." If you we were on a working team, that *was* part of your job. If there was other work to be done, we needed to reallocate it further down the hierarchy or not do it at all. This was, and still is, the only solution to the problem.

When we look at all of our day-to-day activities and ask "Does this really add value? Do I absolutely need to do this?", we often find many ways to save time. We did this with our monthly report. Every month, each department produced this huge report that got e-mailed to fifty to sixty people. It was at least twenty-five pages long. It highlighted everything, ranging from new product development goals to status updates on the various initiatives. Who knows how much work went into creating and reading the reports. But some of us stopped reading them. If we wanted to know whether or not we were leading the market in sales, we'd have an assistant run a report. If we wanted to know how the marketing launch of our new product line was going, we'd call the VP of marketing. This was the information we needed to know. Unfortunately, it was either buried in detail in that twenty-five-page report or not included at all.

Going forward, we've decided to change the monthly report. It will only be two pages long and it will highlight financial metrics that the department heads have agreed on (like sales, growth rate, budget). If a department has reached a major milestone, then it will be covered. However, individual project details by department have been eliminated. Think about it. Creating and then having fifty people read twenty-five often complicated pages versus creating and reading two pages.

If we can identify, recognize, and agree on what people can stop doing, then we won't feel so overwhelmed. We have to focus on the

> important work or we'll never create and adopt the new strategies. So what we need to do now, and what we are trying to put a framework around for the next three or four years, is to continue to identify things like the monthly report and replace them with activities that will move us forward.
>
> For some, making the adjustment will be difficult. We all need to be doing more to help these people.

In "Twenty-Five Pages to Two," one simple change makes a difference. One simple change eliminates what could add up in a year to a thousand hours of wasted managerial effort. The change visibly shows what the boss wants others to do. It is an action that makes his words on the subject more understandable and credible. And it is an action that has consequences that people feel.

The best way to handle the overwork problem is with conscious effort as early in the process as possible. You anticipate the issue rather than suddenly finding it explode in your face. Then you purge your calendar of everything that is a leftover from history and that has no current pressing relevance. You stop the unnecessary Tuesday morning meeting that has been a fixture for five decades. You eliminate the six different kinds of reports that land on your desk, that take time to understand, and that are no longer needed. You use teleconferencing to cut out travel. You no longer attend meetings where your presence is not essential. You kill pet projects that add little to the change effort and yet suck up time and money. You delegate more. You find what can and should be done by others and let them do it. You delegate not only down, but up and sideways. If peers can better do the work, you let them. If bosses can better do the work, you let them. Considerations of prestige—look at all the important work I do—are put aside. Instead, you relentlessly push work off your desk that others can do, should do, and will do. You fight the egotistical tendency most of us have to think we must do something because others cannot.

People are not machines. We need more than maintenance. We need the rejuvenation that comes from sleep, relaxation, and fun off the job. Everyone engaged in a big effort to change a company, a department, or a work group should probably have a banner above the mirror in his or her bathroom at home, a banner to be seen every morning and night that says "Dying will not help."

Our Favorite Step 7 Story

This is *creative*.

The Street

From Jack Jacobs

We had made substantial steps forward in terms of improving customer service, a key element of our new vision. We improved our percentage of on-time and complete shipments from 50 percent to 99 percent, even though 50 percent is pretty much standard in our industry. Our success not only helped our customers; it also helped demonstrate that we were on track. Unfortunately, although improving our delivery percentages so dramatically was a huge win for us, it also suddenly left us open to renewed complacency. The question was, What do we do next?

As it turned out, the changes we made to improve delivery time actually provided us an opportunity to further our vision and values and keep the change rolling. We had removed all our on-site inventory and shifted responsibility for it to our suppliers. The result was we had thousands of square feet in the manufacturing facility that had no use. You walked into our facility and it looked more like an empty warehouse than an assembly line. That's how much space we opened up. We immediately started looking for new materials to store there. Given all the manufacturing we did throughout the southeast, we figured that shouldn't be difficult. We began looking around for other raw materials to put in our new space, things like lumber, steel sheets, plastic rollers, steel pins, and so forth.

Then one of our designers approached me with a brainstorm. "Why don't we use the space to expand the offices?" At the time, we had in the facility a few offices for plant management. But by and large, we housed managers at headquarters, which was about a five-minute drive away. This was not surprising given the plant was one of those boxy, windowless buildings that provided shelter from the elements but little else. We started to think about options for turning the space into offices for all our plant administrative staff and managers.

Given my preoccupation with making sure the change continued, I went back to our vision to see if redesigning the factory fit into the larger change program. What I found was the concept of community. We were committed to building community, believing that we would gain strength and competitive advantage by uniting the thousands of people that work for us. What I realized was that redesigning the manufacturing facility might provide an opportunity to address the whole notion of community. So I threw the question out to our design team. "How can we reconfigure the plant in a way that strengthens community and visibly continues our change program?" What they came up with was truly brilliant.

We decided that community could be strengthened if we found a way to increase the interaction between office workers and line workers. We wondered if we could somehow do this with the available space in the plant. As we thought about this, we got more and more ambitious. What started as a simple idea quickly morphed into a more complicated, awesome idea. We decided to shift the manufacturing line to the center of the factory and then wrap a broad corridor around it. The ceiling of the corridor would be covered with glass so that even on the most cloudy winter days there is light flooding in.

On the other side of the corridor we would wrap our administrative offices. So basically the factory would be in the middle, the offices on the outside, and in between we'd have this broad corridor.

Next we decided to put all the common-use rooms like washrooms, coffee rooms, etc., off of the main corridor so that they would be shared by both office workers and factory workers. For factory workers to use the shared washrooms, they would have to come out of the factory and walk along the corridor. The same is true for the office people. As a result both groups not only share the same facilities but also share the corridor. So there would be constant intermingling. Everyone in the facility would need to use this corridor to get to his or her respective areas.

In fact, the corridor became so well traveled that it was dubbed The Street. The Street is superbly conducive to the mingling of the factory and the office employees. In the coffee room, the restroom, the meeting room, it brings us together. It provides a chance for us to let our hair down. If that doesn't build community, I don't know what does.

So we've managed to not only make more efficient use of the space provided from our first change, we've been able to use that space to build community and ultimately reinforce and continue our change efforts, and to do so in a very visible way. Nobody could miss this. To some degree we were lucky. But the key was a team of people that saw that this is what we should focus on. And we did.

Think of all the ways the people in "The Street" could have pursued the collaboration theme. The most obvious would have been a new program. There might have been speeches, workshops, perhaps a change on the performance appraisal form. All this could have helped, but it would have encountered a workforce tired of change and an employee base whose sense of urgency had sunk. Under those conditions, people often throw up their hands, convince themselves that enough of the vision is complete, declare victory, and resist new programs, no matter how well designed.

The change effort in "The Street" succeeds not because it directly creates collaboration or new collaboration norms. It works because everyone *sees* the company building a space, at some cost, that makes it much easier for employees of all sorts to interact, work together, and be together. This gives huge credence to vague, lofty, visionary ideas like "We should collaborate more." The Street works because the blue collar and office employees see each other often enough for mutual negative stereotyping to decrease. "My goodness, he's human too, wears clothes, speaks English, doesn't eat children for lunch." A decrease in negative stereotyping increases the chances of collaboration. So the achievement of the vision moves along. Another wave of change passes. The company moves nearer to the end of the process. And the firm has an innovative, twenty-first-century, the-PR-guys-are-going-to-love-it work space.

Don't Let Up

Continue with wave after wave of change, not stopping until the vision is a reality, despite seemingly intractable problems.

WHAT HELPS

- Aggressively ridding yourself of work that wears you down—tasks that were relevant in the past but not now, tasks that can be delegated
- Looking constantly for ways to keep urgency up
- Using new situations opportunistically (as in "The Street") to launch the next wave of change
- As always—show 'em, show 'em, show 'em

WHAT DOES NOT HELP

- Developing a rigid four-year plan (be more opportunistic)
- Convincing yourself that you're done when you aren't
- Convincing yourself that you can get the job done without confronting some of the more embedded bureaucratic and political behaviors
- Working so hard you physically and emotionally collapse (or sacrifice your off-the-job life)

STORIES TO REMEMBER

- PE Ratios
- The Merchant of Fear
- Reducing Twenty-Five Pages to Two
- The Street

STEP 8

Make Change Stick

TRADITION IS A POWERFUL FORCE. Leaps into the future can slide back into the past. We keep a change in place by helping to create a new, supportive, and sufficiently strong organizational culture. A supportive culture provides roots for the new ways of operating. It keeps the revolutionary technology, the globalized organization, the innovative strategy, or the more efficient processes working to make you a winner.

Change Can Be Fragile

Successful change is more fragile than we often think, or wish to think. All parents have at one time walked into a room of unruly children, stopped the foolishness, and restored order, only to discover that the order disappeared soon after the children were again alone. This is the making-change-stick problem in a very basic form.

Making it stick can be difficult in any sphere of life. If this challenge is not well met at the end of a large-scale change process, enormous effort can be wasted.

The Boss Went to Switzerland

From John Harris

We had worked very hard to create a way of operating that wasn't like your typical slow, bureaucratic enterprise. We didn't have bosses reporting to bosses reporting to more bosses. Instead of five levels in the hierarchy—not uncommon for this type of business—we cut it to three. Instead of four layers of supervision, we had two. This allowed us to react quickly, and we did. We didn't have to wait while messages went through more hands. We didn't have to wait while decisions bounced back and forth between levels. People were clearly accountable and empowered. They were down in the operations making decisions. If a manager in California decided that we needed to revise the advertising campaign for Friskies in that market, he did that without coming to me.

At times, we had to fight to keep the formal structure needed to support all this. There would be this conversation where someone from headquarters would come and say to me, "So and so needs to have more people responsibility. He needs to have a manager reporting to

him. He's a high-potential person and we've got to develop him."
Now, developing people is essential, but this was not the way we
were doing it, should do it, or could do it without killing our lean and
fast organization. So our response would be, "Well, he has responsibility for marketing pet food in California and he needs to manage
relationships with people across several divisions to get that job
done." And they'd say, "Yes, but to be a VP you need to have ten
people reporting to you." Of course, if we did this, it would mean
creating a VP-level position and hiring more managers.

I also used to have conversations that went something like, "The
organization has grown, so we need to add someone to police what's
going on. We need to have systems to manage them and we need a
VP to do that." This typically came from well-intentioned HR or
Finance staff who were trying to design an organization that pre-
vents people from making mistakes. But that is no good. We needed,
and had created, a sense of responsibility and accountability and
empowerment. We had people making decisions close to the operations. They made mistakes occasionally, but not many, and they
learned from the ones they made. What we didn't need was people
conforming to all the rules.

Then I got transferred to Switzerland.

One of the things that we do to further develop people is send them
for a period of time to our headquarters in Switzerland. So off I went.

I was supposed to be gone five years. That's the time for an
assignment like the one I had. But after three, the results in my former division had dropped so much that I couldn't believe it. How
do results collapse in a good organization in three years? How do
you take an organization that moves pretty fast, where decisions
are made where they need to be made, that has good people, and
go from good to bad results that quickly in an industry that is not
in trouble? How? Swiss management sent me hurrying back to
California.

Back in the U.S. I found a different organization, no longer lean and
fast with people accountable. After being gone only three years, two

levels had been added to the organizational structure. A VP of operations had been assigned and a senior VP too. This in turn created a geometric expansion of people. You add a VP and suddenly you've got to have administrative assistants. You've also got to hire a bunch of managers to report to him. Pretty soon a lean three-layer structure is a fat multilayered structure. Pretty soon everything starts to slow down. Decisions are made at the wrong spot. And that's exactly what I found when I returned to California.

At first it shocked me how fast things reverted to the way they were, but now I see what happened. The person they chose to replace me did not share my vision with respect to running a lean organization. He was satisfied to mirror the organizational structure in many of the company's other divisions. He was probably even rewarded for doing so. I know I had to fight to keep things lean. There were only one or two people behind the shift backward, but that's all it took. As soon as I left, they changed the structure, added the levels, and began operating in a different way. I honestly didn't believe that what we created could be so easily undone once I left.

Now I'm back. We've cut the levels out again. We've cut SG&A to get us leaner, but I see we must do more. I think the only way we can get the vision, the philosophy, embedded is to change the whole way we do business, to link the vision to everything the division does, to mentor individuals who share the vision, and more. It's got to be driven in deeper. It can't be dependent on just me to make it happen, to keep it going the right way.

Change is often held in place solely by a guiding team, a central player in such a team (as in this case), a compensation system, an organizational structure, initial enthusiasm over the results created by the changes, or even less. It may not seem that way. You may think you have built a sturdy house, yet not notice that the walls are being held in place by the construction crew.

Eventually, the crew leaves and gravity takes over. In large-scale change efforts, gravity is the traditional organizational culture.

Culture is a complex concept. For our purposes here, it means the norms of behavior and the shared values in a group of people. It's a set of common feelings about what is of value and how we should act. A good test of whether something is embedded in a culture is if our peers, without really thinking, find ways to nudge us back to group norms when we go astray. The keys are *peers*—that is, a group activity—and *not really thinking,* which means behavior with roots deeper than rational thought.

All the time, we see evidence of culture and its power. In a restaurant, most of us do not make a mess, even though we could and even though it takes a little more time and energy to make sure we don't drop food on the floor. We use a napkin instead of just wiping our hands on the tablecloth. Do we rationally calculate that napkins are good for us because they keep grease off our clothing? If that were true, we would also use bibs. We don't, because using napkins is a habit and, more important, is part of our culture. If we violate that norm and keep using various parts of the tablecloth to wipe our hands and mouths, others in the restaurant will give us unpleasant looks, the service might slow down or speed up to an uncomfortable level because the waiters are appalled, or our dinner companions might not ask us out again. At work, if we showed up naked, we would get an even stronger cultural backlash from everyone, even though there is probably nothing in the HR guidelines that forbids the lack of clothing.

In large-scale change efforts, we use the power of culture to help make a transformation stick. In one way, this is easy. In another, it's extremely difficult. It's difficult because, most of the time, creating a new norm means that you need to change old ones that are deeply embedded. After a few thousand years, try altering the clothes-at-work norm. Yet, in another sense, creating a new culture is easy because it happens naturally as long as there is continuity of behavior and success over a sufficient period of time. That's just the way culture is. You see this most clearly in start-up situations. An entrepreneur creates a new way of operating and it succeeds. If his or her people don't lose the formula despite ego-boosting success, after a few decades a strong enough culture will develop that the entrepreneur's presence will no longer be required.

You can be too successful in creating new cultures. Sometimes entrepreneurs leave norms and shared values that are cement-like, so that when the world changes the organization has great difficulty adjusting. But the problem we face today is rarely the creation of new cultures that are too strong. The problem is usually the opposite. Employee turnover, business pressures, disruptive crises, or bosses going to Switzerland undermine fragile cultures, never allowing them to grow sufficient roots.

New Employee Orientation

Employee turnover can be especially disruptive. When people who strongly exemplify a new culture leave, that culture can go out the door with them. When people are brought into an organization, they bring with them different cultures. In either case, a new way of operating can remain fragile or can degenerate—unless specific actions are taken to deal with the problem.

The Path to the Patient

From Dr. Thomas Rossi

Every employee knows that we discover, develop, and introduce new drugs and that a successful drug is going to benefit the company. But knowing why we do well, why we don't do well, and how successful we are was not something that was intuitively obvious to everybody a couple of years ago. That's because the drugs we launch *don't* fail. We wouldn't launch a bad drug. So if you went around two years ago and asked people in our department whether or not we were successful, they'd say, "Of course. Every drug we introduce helps people, so of course we're adding value to R&D and the company at large."

Just because the drugs that we *do* bring to market are successful doesn't mean that there weren't problems along the way. What our people weren't seeing is that, on average, we were spending 50 percent more per drug than necessary to get it launched. What they weren't seeing is that it was taking us five to six years to get a new drug on the market, instead of three. Why didn't they see this? Because they never came out of their silos. I know *silo* is an overused term nowadays, but it really was reality for us. We had people from a multitude of different scientific disciplines working in their own little worlds, studying their own little piece of science. If they were a part of stage 1 testing, then they performed an initial assessment of the drug, period. They didn't bother to coordinate with the person who did level 3 testing, where we were losing our money on thousands of full-blown patient screenings. Had the testing level 1 and 3 scientists worked together earlier to figure out which drugs were worth the patient screening, we wouldn't have lost as much money on unnecessary work. We've been fixing that.

Our vision has been "to become industry leaders in creating value from R&D." To achieve that, we introduced a full-blown change initiative to pull employees out of their silos and get them focused on their role within the bigger R&D process. We raised urgency by helping people understand where we were underperforming and how we could improve as a whole unit. We got leadership support from the parent organization up front. We involved real up-and-comers from R&D to spearhead the initiative in their areas. We had countless communication events. We had training sessions on the whole R&D process. All this has led to much improvement. But lately, we've been working on the more important piece, which is maintaining all of the change that we've made—making it a way of life.

We can't have new employees come in and reintroduce a silo mentality, which happens *very* easily because most of our hires have spent their lives in silos. So we have thought very carefully about how we introduce new hires to the department. This starts with our orientation program. It's a day-long event held right here at headquarters to help people learn more about drug development. It works with a series of video clips that show new people how we are increasingly doing it, and the values behind those practices.

The video starts with a computer graphic of a highway. As you look at the map you see that it's titled "Path to the Patient." As you go through the highway you take exits. Here's an exit into the world of drug discovery, over there is an exit to development. Before you go on the highway, you hear a few words from the chairman. He explains his view of the pharmaceutical world from the business department: "Here's what we're trying to accomplish." In the last session I attended, I heard a scientist lean over to the woman next to him and say, "In my old department [in a different company] no one even knew who the chairman was!"

There are speeches like the CEO's throughout the video. You exit into "discovery" and there's a scientist talking about the testing process. "Hello. I'd like to introduce you to a robot that we work with to help with some of the initial drug screening. It's able to analyze the compounds in the drug and tell us some of the potential warnings—drug interaction advice, etc. . . . ." Then you're back on the highway and you veer off into product launch. There, you meet a manager who tells about a telephone conversation with someone from phase 3 testing. "I get a phone call from my friend about a new drug that can help patients suffering from epilepsy. They've been screening patients and it looks like a go. So I get a head start on the product launch. I track the drug performance in patient screening, talk to people out in the field, assess the market readiness. . . . ."

The entire orientation, video and presentations included, introduces new hires to our emerging, nonsilo R&D. Now you hear a new hire working on development one week into the job saying, "I already called the people in testing and told them to prepare that robot of theirs because we have another discovery on the way."

We also show new employees (and old ones too) video clips of actual patients who have benefited from drugs we have introduced in the last five years. This helps people understand the end result and it connects our work to personal values. One clip shows a young girl who we helped because we discovered the drug she uses for her epilepsy. She was suffering from maybe sixty, seventy epileptic seizures a day. She couldn't go to school, couldn't study, could hardly even talk. No existing medicine worked, conventional therapy had no effect, but our drug helped. "Thank you," she says, "for letting me be a kid again." This was real, no BS. Believe me when I say that I'm not the first to get choked up by this video. You look around the table and everyone has a tear in their eye, or a smile on their face. It makes you proud to work here, proud to be a part of something great. It sounds sappy, but it's true.

Another way we keep new people focused on the entire R&D process is through the interactive education available on our intranet. You can study at your own pace, but there's a test at the end. The idea is that everyone has to demonstrate that they have some business proficiency around the R&D process. A manager who works on drug discovery just told me that one of his employees finished the test before him and was educating him on how the department could work better with the development group! Apparently she said something like, "Why don't you go check out our intranet site to learn a little bit more about what they're doing over in development. We might be able to coordinate some of our findings a bit earlier."

With this type of effort, we are trying to help new people learn the new way we are doing things, and, through them, ingraining it deeper into everyday life around here.

If all this were done with insincerity, it could have felt like propaganda and would have failed. Even if done well, cynics may have hated it. But the firm probably did not go out of its way to hire cynics. And most of us assume the best and put much of our cynicism aside at the beginning of a new job.

The employee orientation program in "The Path" had four key characteristics:

1. It introduced the R&D group's new ways of operating.

2. It relied heavily on video. New hires could see real employees talking about their work and hear them tell real stories about what they were doing.

3. It used animation creatively to show concretely what is usually discussed in very abstract ways ("We integrate closely the stages of the process"). Because it was done well, the animation was memorable in a way that a traditional briefing is rarely memorable.

4. The video showed a core value in the new culture and did so dramatically with a heartfelt message from a real customer.

With this sort of orientation, compelling visions provoke feelings that help new employees behave "correctly" faster. The group's performance stays at its new level or grows. Continuity of action and success help embed the new behavior deeper into the culture.

The Promotions Process

Another way that a fragile culture can be reinforced is through the promotions process. The right promotions make those people who truly reflect the new norms more influential, thus strengthening those norms.

Promoting the Thirty-Something

From Arthur Sulzberger Jr.

That we have changed our business as much as we have in the last decade is an extraordinary tribute to some of our employees. Over a period of about six years we became a national newspaper, reaching hundreds of thousands and possibly millions of readers outside of our previous geographical base in New York. This meant we had to significantly expand our distribution, circulation, and printing facilities. This meant we had to win advertising contracts in a new way, to consistently help our people believe and achieve the goal of being "national" rather than "local." We had to do this despite having tried and failed to make this type of expansion before, on many occasions.

Through all this, one of the things I've learned is that after you have clarity about where you want to go, once you have communicated that, and once you see real successes in acting by the new rules, nothing helps them to stick better, and nothing helps to create the new culture faster, than promoting out of the hierarchy.

When we were looking for a new head of planning a few months back, there were a number of candidates at the "right" level in the hierarchy who traditionally would have been most likely to get the job. They were good people, but they didn't always demonstrate the new culture, what we call the Rules of the Road. They had been ingrained in the old school, and despite all the changes we had made, they still found it easier or more comfortable to act in ways that supported the past, not the future.

Collaboration is one of the Rules of the Road, but we still had plenty of candidates for promotion who were used to making decisions unilaterally. After all, it's easier and it happens faster, but it's not one of our new Rules. We know that making decisions the old way keeps the hierarchy firmly in place, undermines what we have achieved, and will prevent our business from flourishing in the future. When people at the senior levels can act this way, it encourages others to slide back to the old tradition.

So for the head of planning position, we pulled up Denise Warren. She was a "thirty-something." She was working a flexible schedule. This was considered a "big deal" in our organization. A person that young! A flexible work schedule?! But that decision was a good one for us because it was based on Denise's ability to demonstrate the Rules of the Road while also achieving long-range goals.

We are getting better at recognizing these people and promoting them. Obviously, we have to be careful to pick people who have the skills to do the job. This requires a good process that looks for many different attributes in a candidate. We have to be very careful that we do not create unnecessary animosity among those not selected, or those who had expected a friend would be selected. If people buy into the vision, if you are clear enough about why you are doing what you are doing, and if your rationale is right, most employees will understand even if they are surprised at first.

We have put our stake in the ground with regard to the new ways of operating, approaches that have helped us and that will be important as we go forward. The more people who demonstrate these approaches, and allow others to demonstrate them, then the more chance we have of making them stick.

By putting into positions of power people who have absorbed a new culture, you create an increasingly solid and stable foundation. As long as they are not disliked, which creates anger, any new hire or boss who fits the new norms can help. But promotions into senior managerial jobs help the most because of the power and visibility of those positions.

A cycle can develop. A stronger norm of making the right kind of promotion decisions leads to better (and very visible) advancement choices, which leads to those who embrace the new culture feeling more empowered, which leads to more of the right kind of behavior, which leads to continuing or better business success, which leads to a more ingrained set of new norms, which leads to the right kind of advancement decisions, and so on.

The Power of Emotion

Throughout this book, we have talked about the power of feelings in making a big change happen. A number of times we have told stories about the power of videotape to hit the feelings. Here's one final, excellent example.

The Home Mortgage

From Terry Pearce, Evelyn Dilsaver, and Dan Leemon

We have grown employment by 25 percent a year for the past six years. What this has meant is that only one in four of our people lived all the way through the change. Despite our success, the culture was at risk of being diluted. So we decided to involve the entire company in a "reexamination of our values," this time in the context of the Internet. We called this event Visionquest. It lasted for four hours one Saturday morning and involved all 40,000 people in our organization around the world. We were all hooked together by satellite.

In our company we have always spent a lot of time gathering stories of our values in action. At one senior management dinner we attended two years before Visionquest, we talked about a number of stories. At the end of the evening each table voted on the ones they liked the best. We decided then and there to use these in new employee orientation and other company events. At Visionquest, we used three of those stories.

One that particularly stands out, because of the reaction it provoked, was about our value of fairness. A video showed the son of one of our customers standing in front of a house. He told us how his parents had been hit by the crash of '87 and owed our company money. The task of collecting these debts fell to one of our vice presidents. He went to southern California to talk with the parents about how they would pay the money back. All they had left was an IRA account with us and their home. Both parents were in their late sixties, and neither was in good health. In the end, an arrangement was made that we would take the equity in the house to settle the debt. By agreement, the couple could live in the house until they no longer needed it, at which time it would revert to us. On the video, the son told viewers that we also agreed they could keep the IRA account as a necessary addition to their retirement fund. Our vice president's empathy and sense of fairness would not allow him to put the parents out of their home.

Now, as stories go, this in itself would have been more than enough to demonstrate what our values are and how we live them. But there was more! On the video, this man told us that a couple of years after the settlement, his father died and his mother continued to live in the house. A few years after that, a fire in that part of southern California burned the house to the ground. We could have taken the insurance money at that point. But appropriately, an entirely different person from the firm assessed the situation in exactly the same way that our vice president had. He helped the woman negotiate a settlement with the insurance company. The house was rebuilt. She moved back into it. When she died five years later, the debt was finally settled. Her son had agreed to make the video for us because he was so grateful that we had cared for them in this way.

I think all of us noticed people in the room respond powerfully to that story. There was one woman who had walked into the conference room, and because it was a Saturday morning, you could tell just by her dress and overall demeanor that she was not particularly happy to be there. After thirty minutes of Visionquest, she put the book down that she had been reading while our CEO did his opening speech. She started to listen. After that particular video she was, like many others, fully engaged in this event. And some people were in tears.

We need to do this sort of thing, and not just once. It has a power that goes far beyond just handing out a statement of our values to all the new hires. It helps all of us remember the special company we have created, a specialness that makes customers want to do business with us and makes great people want to work here.

The firm had done well, in part, because it had made itself into an organization that treated its customers fairly. This had become a part of the culture. But with rapid additions of personnel, that culture, and the behavior it supported, was at risk of becoming severely diluted. So with Visionquest and other means, they tried to help the old-timers and the new, especially the latter, *see* what the firm cared about, *feel* it, and feel good about it. Those group feelings then helped create the behavior and success that strengthened the winning culture.

A Controversial but Very Important Point

To use all of the ideas in this chapter, and to avoid the mistakes, it is essential to understand a fundamental and widely misunderstood aspect of organizational change. In a change effort, culture comes last, not first.

Enterprises often try to shift culture first. The logic is straightforward. If the culture is inward looking, risk averse, and slow, we'll change that first. Then nearly any new vision can be implemented more easily. Sounds reasonable, but it doesn't work that way.

A culture truly changes only when a new way of operating has been shown to succeed over some minimum period of time. Trying to shift the norms and values before you have created the new way of operating does not work. The vision can talk of a new culture. You can create new behaviors that reflect a desired culture. But those new behaviors will not become norms, will not take hold, until the very end of the process.

This reality flies in the face of what you hear in many places today. To some degree the issue is semantics. People say *culture* when what they mean is new behavior, a new way of operating. But if you think this way, you may try to create that new manner of operating immediately, ignoring complacency or an ineffective guiding team. At best you will make it through step 7 and think you are done. Then you will fail.

We can do better than that. Much better. This isn't rocket science. Once you see what works, once you have an optimistic sense that you can help create better organizations, it's amazing what can happen.

Make Change Stick

Be sure the changes are embedded in the very culture of the enterprise so that the new way of operating will stick.

WHAT WORKS

- Not stopping at step 7—it isn't over until the changes have roots
- Using new employee orientation to compellingly show recruits what the organization really cares about
- Using the promotions process to place people who act according to the new norms into influential and visible positions
- Telling vivid stories over and over about the new organization, what it does, and why it succeeds
- Making absolutely sure you have the continuity of behavior and results that help a new culture grow

WHAT DOES NOT WORK

- Relying on a boss or a compensation scheme, or anything but culture, to hold a big change in place
- Trying to change culture as the first step in the transformation process

STORIES TO REMEMBER

- The Boss Went to Switzerland
- The Path to the Patient
- Promoting the Thirty-Something
- The Home Mortgage

We See, We Feel, We Change

TURBULENCE WILL NEVER CEASE. THE best evidence says that winning organizations will continue to deal with this fact by following the eight-step process of adaptation and transformation. The single biggest challenge in the process is changing people's behavior. The key to this behavioral shift, so clear in successful transformations, is less about analysis and thinking and more about seeing and feeling.

Albert Schweitzer once said, "Example is not the main thing influencing others. It is the only thing."

Thinking and Feeling

Clear thinking is a critical part of large-scale change, whether in a big organization or a small department. Figuring out the right strategy is perhaps the most obvious example. Locating information to be used in raising urgency is another. Selecting possibilities for short-term wins is still another. But look at story after story of highly successful change methods and you find a pattern that is closer to the heart of the matter. People are sensitive to the emotions that undermine change, and they find ways to reduce those feelings. People are sensitive to the emotions that facilitate change, and they find ways to enhance those feelings. This is true throughout all eight stages of a process that helps organizations leap forward.

The emotions that undermine change include anger, false pride, pessimism, arrogance, cynicism, panic, exhaustion, insecurity, and anxiety. The facilitating emotions include faith, trust, optimism, urgency, reality-based pride, passion, excitement, hope, and enthusiasm.

Successful change leaders identify a problem in one part of the change process, or a solution to a problem. Then they show this to people in ways that are as concrete as possible. They show with a vehicle you can see, hear, or touch. This means a demonstration with gloves rather than a report on gloves. Change leaders make their points in ways that are as emotionally engaging and compelling as possible. This means a competition in Bali that has entertainment and tears rather than a cerebral event in a New York conference room. Change leaders show people the truth with a variety of creative live presentations and events. They use videotape of both angry and joyful customers. They rely on vivid stories, even tales of bodies in living rooms. They model in their actions what they need from others, even when it is risky to stand in front of former adversaries in war. They make sure a result is visible on bulletin boards or on paper for a state senator. They

See, Feel, Change

See

Identify a problem, or a solution to a problem, in one stage of a change process, and then help people visualize this in a way that enables a helpful change in behavior. Show people in a way that is as concrete as possible—touchable, feelable, seeable, especially the latter (as in "Gloves"). Show the problem or solution in an emotionally engaging, dramatic, vivid, and compelling way ("The Plane," "Worldwide Competition"). Use live presentations ("Q&A"), modeling ("General Mollo," "Blues/Greens"), video ("The Merchant of Fear," "Home Mortgage"), stories ("The Body"), physical environment ("The Street"), visible results ("New Navy," "The Senator"), new demands placed on people ("Retooling"), and old demands taken away ("My Portal"). Give the show an afterburner via physical symbols that people see each day ("Portrait Gallery"), stories that are told and retold ("I Survived"), or ongoing role modeling ("Promoting").

Feel

The dramatic, vivid visualizations catch people's attention, reducing emotions that undermine a sensible change—feelings of anger, complacency, false pride, pessimism, confusion, panic, cynicism. "Seeing" increases emotions that facilitate a needed change regarding some valid idea—feelings of passion, faith, trust, pride, urgency, hope (and fear, if quickly converted into any of the others).

Change

Different feelings—a change of heart—transform behavior. The new behavior helps groups and organizations effectively move through the eight steps and leap into a prosperous future.

change the context so what people see is different: new physical environments with different architecture; new, much shorter reports; new painting-picture approaches to planning; new jobs inspecting the very problems that need to be solved. They provide a means for the show to live on with physical objects that people see each day—aircraft and portraits—or with vivid stories that are told and retold. But whatever the method, they supply valid ideas that go deeper than the conscious and analytic part of our brains—ideas with an emotional impact. The feelings change behavior, and with this change people are able to move through the eight necessary stages of large-scale change despite often huge difficulties. People manage to leap into a better future, often despite initial skepticism that such a leap is possible or even necessary. People succeed to the point of producing small miracles.

To some degree, this pattern is related to the structure of the brain. The part that deals with sophisticated analysis has come late in evolutionary terms. The bigger, hard-wired section sends information directly from the senses to the emotions, which then instigate action. To some degree, the pattern is also related to the nature of large-scale change in an age of turbulence. Analytical tools require known parameters and work much less well with uncertainty.

At a gut level, we all know the see-feel-change method. We've all observed it and experienced it many times. But we know it less well at a conscious level. We rarely tell each other about it, talk about it, or teach it in formal settings. This will change, because the needs of an accelerating world will force it to change.

More Than a Few Heroes

In a more stable era, the sort of transformation discussed in this book is not of great importance. The name of the game is securing a strong position and holding onto it. Build a big moat around a castle, keep the moat repaired, keep the army trained, and stay put. As the rate of change increases, however, the approaches and tactics described here become more important. Someone needs to understand these ideas and provide leadership in using them well. As the rate of change increases still more, one or two *some-ones* is no longer enough. More people must appreciate the need for bigger leaps and what is required to take them successfully. Otherwise, you won't be able to push urgency up fast enough, form the right guiding teams at various levels in the organization, or communicate the vision widely yet quickly. As the rate of change increases still more, so does the need for more change-sophisticated people.

CEOs, division presidents, and other major players in organizations are still critical. Try to run around them and you will suffer failure. Try to do anything in those situations except work on step 1, raising their urgency, and frustration is almost inevitable. But perfect CEOs are never enough except in very small enterprises.

Today, in many older and more protected industries, if 1 percent of the workforce understands the ideas in this book, an organization can probably move fast enough. In a small company with 100 employees, that would mean just the CEO. In a huge company with 50,000 employees, 1 percent means 500 people. Small companies are much more likely to have a change-savvy CEO than big ones are to have 500 change-savvy managers, which is one reason the small companies are faster and more agile.

But when the rate of change is accelerating, then what?

In a turbulent world, the requirement for change is ongoing. Imagine needing to keep urgency up and complacency, fear, and anger down all the time and throughout the organization. Imagine needing to have groups guiding change efforts all the time and throughout the enterprise. Imagine the demand to develop visions and strategies for all the changes, to communicate volumes of information to everyone, to keep batting obstacles out of the way throughout the organization. To succeed in that world, how many people in an enterprise must see change as a part of their jobs? How many of us must understand change well enough to help with the waves of new product lines, mergers, reorganizations, the e-world, process reengineering, or leaps of any kind? How many of us need some minimum capability in addition to analysis-think-act tactics? Reasonable people can argue about what these numbers should be, but the figures surely are very large. Most organizations have less than half of what they need today, and many enterprises have only a fraction.

Imagine, for a moment, four enterprises, each with about 5,000 employees. The organizations are all in the same industry and are similar in many ways except one. In the first, pretty much everyone sees the head of the organization as "The Change Leader." The boss thinks this way too, and he is the only person who even tries to take the sorts of actions examined in this book. In the second enterprise, a few dozen managers are thought of as change leaders. These men and women try to march through the eight steps in their parts of the organization. They use the see-feel-change tactics shown in the stories throughout this book. In the third, a few hundred managers are expected to lead change in some aspect of their work. A few hundred understand the centrality of emotion. Their language and behavior follows accordingly. Dorothy supplies change leadership on the new Crain project with help from Tad and Bill. Jerry's team provides change leadership for the vision in the Parts Group. John, Meri, and Gunther serve as change leaders in the Boise office.

Imagine that in the forth and final organization, more than half the workforce is expected to provide change leadership in some arena. Most of this "leadership" will be modest. It may focus on only one of the steps. But it is change leadership. And suppose that in this fourth organization, most accept the challenge. Among 5,000 employees, that means at least 2,501 people are helping the enterprise deal with a volatile age. In a world that lurches left or right at 170 miles an hour, which of these four firms will win?

But can large numbers of people realistically help us deal with turbulent times? If you think about the job in Herculean terms, obviously not. If you think about the job of leading change in terms of helping give direction to, or energizing, a part of one of the eight steps, then why not?

Why can't a twenty-four-year-old salesperson take the initiative, bring into the firm information about a new opportunity or threat, and use the information creatively to create a show-'em presentation that increases urgency among a boss and a few peers? Why can't a twenty-eight-year-old engineer be an effective part of a group that guides the development of a new product line? Why can't a fifty-five-year-old administrative assistant buried deep in the hierarchy use some passionate discussions to help effectively communicate a vision to her peers? Why can't nearly anyone be the key player in planning for and creating a short-term win? Does human chemistry stop us from dealing with emotions competently? Probably not.

Although told very succinctly by middle managers or senior executives, most of the stories in this book, if presented as detailed thirty-page Harvard Business School cases, would also have in them the likes of that twenty-four-year-old salesperson or the fifty-five-year-old administrative assistant. Probably none of these people would look like "leaders" in a traditional sense. But all help provide very real change leadership.

We need more of these people, and there is no reason we cannot have more. We need more people doing what they already do, but better—and there is no reason why that also is not possible. We've seen this throughout history. The needs of World War II forced a bureaucratic military to miraculously produce a handful of great leaders, hundreds of good leaders, and tens of thousands of people who performed leadership acts. In many ways our emerging challenge is greater than World War II. Our response can be greater as well.

STORY INDEX

Step Listing

ABOUT THE AUTHORS

JOHN P. KOTTER is a graduate of MIT and Harvard. He joined the Harvard Business School faculty in 1972. In 1980, at the age of thirty-three, he was voted tenure and a full professorship.

Kotter is the author of *John P. Kotter on What Leaders Really Do* (1999), *Matsushita Leadership* (1997), *Leading Change* (1996), *The New Rules* (1995), *Corporate Culture and Performance* (1992), *A Force for Change* (1990), *The Leadership Factor* (1988), *Power and Influence* (1985), *The General Managers* (1982), and five other books published in the 1970s. His books have been reprinted in eighty foreign language editions, and total sales are approaching two million copies. He has also created two executive videos, "Leadership" (1991) and "Corporate Culture" (1993), and an educational CD-ROM (1998) based on *Leading Change*. His articles in the *Harvard Business Review* have sold a million and a half copies.

Kotter's honors include an Exxon Award for Innovation in Graduate Business School Curriculum Design and a Johnson, Smith & Knisely Award for New Perspectives in Business Leadership. In 1996, *Leading Change* was named the #1 management book of the year by *Management General* and in 1998, *Matsushita Leadership* won the *Financial Times*/Booz•Allen & Hamilton

Global Business Book Award for biography/autobiography. In October 2001, *Business Week* magazine rated Kotter the #1 "leadership guru" in America based on a survey they conducted of 504 enterprises.

Kotter lives in Cambridge, Massachusetts and in Ashland, New Hampshire with his wife, Nancy Dearman, and his children, Caroline and Jonathan. He can be reached at jkotter@hbs.edu.

DAN S. COHEN is a Principal with Deloitte Consulting where he focuses his consulting activities on large-scale organizational transformation. He heads Deloitte Consulting's Global Energy Change Leadership practice and led the development of the firm's Global Change Leadership Methodology. He has provided consulting support to a number of the Fortune 100 Companies such as Exxon-Mobil, Baker Hughes, Dell, The Coca-Cola Company, and Reliant Energy. Prior to consulting, he worked in the manufacturing, financial, and real estate industries for over fifteen years in various executive human resource positions. In addition to his consulting work, Cohen has lectured on organizational behavior at the University of Detroit, Ohio State University, Miami University, and Southern Methodist University. He obtained his B.A. at Adelphi University, M.A. at University of Detroit, and his Ph.D. at Ohio State.

Cohen lives in Plano, Texas with his wife Ronnie. He can be reached at dacohen@dc.com.